ROMAN FORTS IN THE FYLDE

Excavations at Dowbridge Kirkham

C Howard–Davis
K Buxton

With contributions by

J Carrott, B Dickinson, L Gidney, A Hall,
L Hird, M Issitt, H Kenward,
F Large, B McKenna, J Mills, D Shotter

CENTRE FOR NORTH WEST REGIONAL STUDIES
LANCASTER UNIVERSITY

i

Roman Forts in the Fylde:
Excavations at Dowbridge, Kirkham

Published by
The Centre for North West Regional Studies
Lancaster University 2000

ISBN 1-86220-086-6

Printed by
Central Print Unit, Lancaster University

Editors
Rachel Newman and David Shotter
Design, layout and production
Andrea Scott

Front Cover: Reconstruction of a Roman fort by David Vale

Abbreviations

CIL *Corpus Inscriptionum Latinarum*

EH   English Heritage

LUAU Lancaster University Archaeological Unit

RIC   Mattingly *et al* 1923-84

Contributors

Jo Mills and Brenda Dickinson undertook analysis on the samian pottery.

Louise Hird compiled the coarse pottery report.

David Shotter produced the coin report.

Louisa Gidney reported on the animal bone.

Environmental work was undertaken by John Carrott, Alan Hall, Michael Issitt, Harry Kenward, Frances Large and Barrie McKenna, all of the Environmental Archaeology Unit at York University.

CONTENTS

LIST OF ILLUSTRATIONS

Figures

Plates

Tables

Summary

The site at Dowbridge, Kirkham (SD 424 322) was excavated in early 1994 in advance of re-development. Both the excavation and post-excavation was generously funded by Wimpey Homes Holdings Limited. Excavation revealed at least four phases of activity at the site, beginning in the late first century AD. Phase 1 comprised three possible temporary camps, all short-lived, with the earliest constructed in the late AD 70s, the latest around the turn of the first century. Later (Phase 2) a small signal station/fortlet was constructed on the site, possibly marking landfall in the Ribble estuary. This was replaced around AD 120 (Phase 3) by a larger and more permanent fort with a substantial stone-fronted rampart and a deep defensive ditch which was renewed at least twice during its lifetime. The fort appears to have been abandoned around AD 150, and thereafter slowly fell into disrepair. The final phase of activity (Phase 4) can be placed in the medieval period, when the stone-revetted ramparts seem to have provided a convenient source of building stone and the surrounding area was cultivated.

Acknowledgements

This report has been made possible by the hard work and support of many people. The authors would like to thank everyone concerned in the excavation at Dowbridge Close, including excavation assistants Alison Denton, Karen Miller, Robin Page, Michael Peace, Christopher Swain and Christopher Wild. The surveying and finds supervisor was Ian Miller, who was assisted during the survey by Ian Scott, and with the finds by Stuart Elder. The evaluation was undertaken by David Hodgkinson, who also supervised on site and undertook much of the post-excavation work. Special thanks are also due to Roger Moon, the machine driver.

LUAU management and administration was undertaken by Mark Fletcher, Rachel Newman, Jill Pollard and Sarah Edwards. Jamie Quartermaine acted as the field survey manager and computing support was given by John Dodds. Illustrations were undertaken by Peter Lee and Richard Danks, CAD illustrations were produced by Ian Miller, and samian illustrations were undertaken by Nick Griffith. Final Phase plans for publication were drawn by Emma Carter.

Thanks are also due to Derek Sparks, John Walmsley, Colin Skinner and Jack Lever of Wimpey Homes Holdings Limited, without which this work would not have been possible.

Finally, the authors would like to thank Adrian Olivier (English Heritage), David Shotter (Lancaster University), Ben Edwards (then Lancashire County Archaeologist) and Peter Iles (Lancashire County Archaeological Service) for their advice, and last, but not least, the people of Kirkham for their interest and enthusiasm.

CHAPTER 1
INTRODUCTION

The presence of a Roman fort at Kirkham has been long postulated on the basis of numerous casual finds and reports. Amongst the latter, a series of unpublished amateur excavations in the 1950s and 1960s identified probable Roman features on both sides of the present A584 in the vicinity of Dowbridge. The recognition of substantial ditches and a possible rampart during these excavations confirmed the supposition of a significant Roman fort, but little could be deduced of its size or dating.

Desktop survey in advance of proposed development in the area of Dowbridge Close in late July-early August 1993 (Hodgkinson 1993) described a long but sparse history of archaeological investigations, the most recent of which identified substantial Roman remains in the vicinity of Dowbridge Close and in Myrtle Drive. The seven small trenches excavated in the subsequent programme of evaluation established the presence of Roman remains within the area of proposed development, and consequently the County Archaeological Curator required a full programme of archaeological investigation to be undertaken in advance of development.

Lancaster University Archaeological Unit (LUAU) was commissioned by Wimpey Homes Holdings Limited, to undertake archaeological investigations on the site. The work was undertaken between January and April 1994 (Buxton 1994).

Location

The town of Kirkham (SD 424 322) lies in the southern part of the Fylde, some 12km east of the coast at Blackpool and 5km north of the lower reaches of the River Ribble, at the point where the Dow Brook runs into it at Naze Mount; this also marks the lowest fording point. The present town (Fig 1) is located on the low ridge of glacial moraine which runs westwards across the Fylde from Preston and terminates in low sea cliffs at Blackpool. Modern Kirkham in fact marks the highest point on this ridge at 30.8m OD and thus commands considerable views over the low-lying coastal plain. The Roman fort lies at Dowbridge, towards the eastern extremity of the present town, close to the line of the Dow Brook.

Most of the coastal development to the west is of late date, associated with the growth of Blackpool as a seaside resort in the nineteenth and early twentieth centuries, and there is little doubt that, prior to that development, much of the area was wetland or had only been recently drained (Middleton *et al* 1995). To the east the land rises gently and is markedly drier. South of the Ribble estuary West Lancashire is, again, low-lying and wet with extensive wetlands, most of which remained undrained until the eighteenth century (Middleton and Tooley forthcoming).

Background

The North West Wetlands Survey, undertaken by LUAU and funded by English Heritage, has resulted in a detailed study of the prehistoric and later archaeology and environment of the Fylde (see Middleton *et al* 1995). This, coupled with the earlier work of Tooley (eg Tooley 1980) on the marine transgression series at Lytham, has allowed the fort at Dowbridge to be set within a fairly well-defined prehistoric context.

The area saw relatively intensive activity during the Bronze Age and earlier, with a number of find spots and sites recorded, suggesting, as would seem logical, a preferential distribution along the major rivers and the ridges of higher ground formed by the englacial boulder clay. It is certain that by the Bronze Age such ridges were thickly wooded and surrounded by established and growing peat bogs: mosses at Lytham and Marton Mere lay close to the ridge on which the Kirkham fort was built. Intensive arable exploitation appears to have come late to the area, with some clearance but little cereal cultivation before the late Iron Age/Roman period, suggesting a bleak, rather wet, possibly quite hostile landscape. Presumably the wetland resource was extensively exploited at all periods and the persistence of evidence for clearance without significant cereal cultivation might suggest a general reliance on a shifting pastoralist regime, including sheep (Huckerby 1992, 16), until a relatively late date; it was likely to have been transhumant since, although wetland edges can provide excellent summer grazing, in the winter livestock would be at risk in the treacherous conditions.

Further to the north across the River Wyre, there is evidence for a prehistoric trackway, Kate's Pad (Middleton 1992), suggesting that in the Fylde, as elsewhere, prehistoric groups travelled relatively freely through wetland areas. Such a trackway may have existed closer to Kirkham, in the form of Dane's Pad, although successive attempts to confirm or discredit this trackway have led to some confusion.

The later prehistoric period in this region appears to have been one of marked climatic and environmental decline closely associated with two episodes of marine transgression (Lytham VIII and IX, Tooley 1980), during which sea level rose significantly. Although to a degree cancelled by isostatic recovery, Tooley has suggested that during the Roman period the Mean High Water Mark at Lytham rose by +4.5m, approximately 1m higher than present Mean High Water Spring Tides (*op cit*, 74-86). Such a rise must have significantly altered the aspect of such a low-lying area.

The climatic deterioration towards the end of the Bronze Age seems to have led to a significant reduction in the density of settlement and thus the potential for the generation of wealth amongst remaining groups in the region. Iron Age sites and even chance finds in north Lancashire are, indeed, conspicuous by their absence, although palaeoenvironmental investigations clearly indicate land clearance and the beginnings of cereal cultivation on the Fylde during this period (summarised in Middleton *et al* 1995). It is suggested that the drive towards social change, fuelled by pressure on land and the need to accumulate wealth which characterised the Iron Age elsewhere, was effectively atrophied in this area by the adverse conditions. Thus it is likely that when the Romans arrived at Kirkham there was little, if any, nucleated settlement nearby, nor any other significant socio-economic foci either to exploit or to arrogate to their purposes, and that the fort was in effect a greenfield site, its foundation driven exclusively by Roman tactical considerations.

The sea-level rise charted by Tooley (1980) may well have meant that the Ribble estuary was significantly closer to Kirkham in the Roman period; sea dykes over 1km inland at Clifton Marsh indicate that this is relatively recently reclaimed land, and it is more than likely that a raised sea level would have backed up and flooded at least part of the shallow valley of the Dow Brook towards Kirkham, raising the possibility of direct access from the sea to the fort, a point made by Singleton: 'It [Kirkham] had obvious connections with the Ribble, which at that time must have covered, at least on the tide, the embayment of Freckleton Marsh, and would be within sight of the fort' (Singleton 1980, 8), and also, in a differing context, by Shotter (1984, 7-9). Thus the choice of site at Kirkham might well have reflected a need to establish and secure sea-borne supply routes rather than to guard the lowest ford on the Ribble. In fact, it may be argued that, with a raised sea-level, the Ribble estuary would have been substantially wider at that point. Much of the land on its southern side is today extremely low-lying, around 5m OD, and would then, presumably, have been flooded. In such a case, the significance of this fording point would have been drastically reduced. It is also of note that the next two river crossings, at Walton-le-Dale and Ribchester, are both dominated by substantial, and early, Roman sites. It seems reasonable to suppose that the invading Roman forces, rather than break virgin ground, followed established native routes and often fortified or defended the river crossings which lay on these, which were presumably already well-known and important to the local population. Perversely, this might lend weight to the suggestion that Kirkham looked to the sea for supplies, perhaps serving as an entrepot for the other forts along the Ribble, since it is extremely unlikely that any military commander in their right mind would have chosen to march a vulnerable invasion force north across the vast mosses of West Lancashire to ford a wide and treacherous estuary, when there was an extant crossing point only 10km to the east at Walton-le-Dale.

The site was closely linked physically (by road and river) with the recently excavated site at Walton-le-Dale (Gibbons and Howard-Davis forthcoming) and the cavalry fort at Ribchester (Buxton and Howard-Davis forthcoming). The road, which ran along the northern side of the Ribble, may well have been closer to the line of the river at that time. Evidence from Ribchester in fact suggests that activity at the two forts may have been closely related. When the road from Kirkham to Ribchester fell out of use, apparently in the later second century (presumably when the fort at Kirkham was abandoned), the extramural buildings which had grown up alongside the road at Ribchester fell into swift decline, as if their existence had been reliant on trade or communication between the two forts. Such a suggestion is of interest in that it seems to indicate that the road, rather than the river upon which they both stood, was, at least in the first and second centuries, at least as important as a transport route.

It has also been suggested that the Kirkham fort was intended to control a route across the Fylde (thought by some to be the Dane's Pad) to the elusive *Portus Setantiorum* mentioned by Ptolemy (*Geographia II,* 3, 2) and thought by some to lie on the lower reaches of the Wyre somewhere near Fleetwood (for instance, Dixon 1949). It might, however, be argued that such a line of communication would have been unnecessary if Kirkham itself had easy sea access. The relative ease and speed of sea-borne transport would have made trade and military supply more effective by sea in a series of short coastal journeys between Chester, Kirkham, Fleetwood(?) and Lancaster. The idea that Kirkham may in fact be *Portus Sentantiorum* is not a particularly new one, although it has received little promotion: Whitaker, writing in 1773, pointed out that '...twenty five miles to the norther (*sic*) of the Merſey (*sic*) can carry us only to one place convenient for an harbour, the mouth of the Ribble...' (1773, 175); '...there then Ptolemy has fixed the harbour' (*op cit,* 176); and '...from this name of the Ribble-mouth, Portus Siſtuntiorum the aeſtuary appears to have been employed by the Romans as an harbour for their veſſels' (*op cit,* 177). It must, however, be acknowledged that other scholars, especially Higham (1986, 146-7) would see the Setantii further north, in southern Cumbria.

Kirkham thus can be seen in parallel with Chester and Lancaster to the south and north, as forts close to the mouths of rivers which form the basis of significant communications routes and which were further guarded elsewhere by forts at crossing points. The Roman finds from Over Wyre are sparse (although some have been recovered from Fleetwood and the line of the river Wyre) (Middleton *et al* 1995) and this general absence would seem somewhat anomalous if the mouth of the Wyre accommodated a Roman port even if, as has been suggested

(Dixon 1949), this now lies under water, eroded away by the waters of Morecambe Bay.

Little is known of Kirkham after the Roman period. No evidence illustrates early medieval activity in the locale, even though the settlement was listed in the Domesday Survey (Faull and Stinson 1986; Hinde 1986). This grew into a town (created a borough in 1296; Farrer and Brownbill 1912), the nucleus of which lay slightly to the west of Dowbridge. During the later medieval period the area of the site seems to have been part of the townfields and appears to have been cultivated in some fashion almost until the present day.

History of the Site

Little is known of the chronology or the layout of the Roman fort at Kirkham. Its existence was first deduced by Edward Baines (Harland 1868-70, 482) on the basis of a number of finds in the vicinity (for instance, Plates 1 and 2). Later authors and further finds reinforced his conclusions: Thornber, in 1840, quotes a local schoolmaster's description of a 'square fortress' of 'massy chiselled red sandstone' at Carr Hill (Singleton 1980, 1) and presents evidence for burials on the west bank of the Dow Brook. Several other finds were noted between 1840 and 1849; a tombstone of 'cavalryman and barbarian' type was seen and destroyed when the parish church was rebuilt in 1844 (Croston 1893, 360); a coin hoard was found during the construction of Kirkgate in 1853 (Sutherland 1936, 316-320).

Evidence from earlier excavations is sadly incomplete. In 1928 Burrows (Collingwood and Taylor 1928) investigated a length of Roman road by the Dow Brook and found along with the road a spring 'with many small fragments of waterworn pottery dating from the first and second centuries AD' (Singleton 1980), and what he described as the western abutment of a Roman bridge across the river. In 1938, building works near South Farm produced Roman material, subsequently identified by Professor Eric Birley as first to third century AD in date (Singleton 1980, 3). The clay and turf rampart observed during the construction of RAF married quarters in the 1950s (somewhere on the present site) fired local interest and a local society was formed which excavated intermittently from 1957 to 1964 under the direction of the late Ernest Pickering; although some of the drawings, some summary reports, and some pottery survive, the work was never fully written up. His notes do not survive, but it seems that amongst other features (B Edwards, pers comm), he excavated a substantial defensive ditch with cobbled berm, running north-south, and a remnant of the sandstone revetments of the second century fort.

Subsequently a major opportunity to clarify the archaeology of the fort was missed when the Carr Hill Hotel, in the grounds of which most of the previous excavations took place, was demolished and the site developed for housing (B Edwards, pers comm). Finally, a tiny excavation in 1985 in the garden of a bungalow on Myrtle Drive further demonstrated that a considerable depth of stratified Roman deposits existed. It revealed what might have been part of the eastern defensive ditch of a Roman fort., which was assumed to be of conventional layout and occupied from about the time of the Agricolan advance into the second century and, perhaps, beyond (B Edwards, pers comm).

Academic Objectives

The fort at Kirkham was so little known that any controlled modern excavation was seen as of benefit, particularly when redevelopment would have an adverse impact on the site. A set of research objectives was formulated within the project design in an attempt to use the limited opportunity presented by these excavations to the full. It was envisaged that those objectives should act as a review of Roman activity on the site within both its local and regional context.

The most basic of the research objectives was to confirm the existence of a fort, or successive forts, on the site and to establish a chronology for the foundation and duration of Roman activity. Such investigation was intended to include an attempt to establish the following points: the date, size, shape and purpose of any fort or forts, and any variations through time in these elements. Likewise, any civilian activity and/or pre- or post-Roman activity required characterisation.

Recent work at other Roman sites in the region, especially those on the course of the River Ribble at Walton-le-Dale (Gibbons and Howard-Davis forthcoming) and Ribchester (Buxton and Howard-Davis forthcoming) has enabled the early days of Roman occupation in this area to be explored and placed within a chronological and environmental framework which is now established as pre-dating the conventional Agricolan context. It was recognised that Kirkham could, and should, be placed within this framework, and to this end chronological and functional links between the three sites were sought. Such links were also intended to allow further consideration of the marked lack of Roman presence elsewhere in the Fylde, especially in regard to the continuing discussion of the location of the sea port of *Portus Setantiorum*.

Methodology

The extensive and disparate nature of the excavation at Dowbridge Close, in the face of limited time and finances, necessitated an excavation methodology which utilised a range of rapid modern techniques. In addition, the deep deposits in the better preserved sections of the defensive ditches, along with the waterlogged conditions associated with excavating a clay site in the winter months, necessitated that some ditch sections were excavated entirely by machine as almost instantaneous flooding and/or collapse of the sections made hand excavation impossible. Shoring of these sections, although considered as an option, was rejected on the basis of health and safety.

The site was investigated by the excavation of 29 trenches placed to maximise information recovery (Fig 2). Although trenches were positioned primarily in order to answer specific archaeological questions which presented themselves during the excavation, the location of trenches was also governed by the presence of modern disturbance in the form of housing, roads and fuel tanks, the proximity of trees, and contamination by heating fuel (Plate 3).

In general, trenches fell into one of two categories: large open areas and small trenches opened either to trace the line of specific features already located, or to investigate areas of supposed negative evidence.

Trench A, in the extreme north-east corner of the available area, was intended to allow further investigation of two linear features identified during evaluation (Hodgkinson 1993). Nothing of obvious archaeological interest was seen during the removal of the top and subsoil layers by machine but, as this was the first trench investigated, it was cleaned by hand on several occasions in order to verify the lack of features. Nothing of archaeological significance was found and the remainder of the trench was excavated by machine down to disturbed natural clay, as were the majority of the subsequent trenches.

Trench B, in the south-east corner of the site, was positioned to examine other linear features found during the evaluation. In the event these turned out to be of modern origin. Trenches C and G were opened in the central northern part of the site, just to the east of the main entrance. They were intended to locate and

5

examine sandstone walling found during the evaluation. Trenches D, F, J and K were excavated to the west of Trench A in order to determine the extent of features revealed in the latter. Trenches E, H, L, M and XD were cut on the lower, southern slopes of the site in order to examine potential activity in this area. Trench N was opened initially to investigate the alignment of features associated with the final, stone-built phase of the fort; earlier features were found in the southern part of the trench. Trenches P, Q, R, S, T and U lay to the west of Trench C and the main entrance to the site, and were positioned to establish the western extent of the Roman activity. Trenches O, X, XB, Y and Z were opened to the south of the western area of the stone fort defences and were positioned to investigate features associated with that fort. Finally, Trenches I, V, W and XC were positioned to examine areas presumed to contain little archaeology.

All site recording was undertaken in accordance with the current English Heritage (Centre for Archaeology) practice. Recording was *proforma*-based, with records transcribed into an Access database for subsequent manipulation. Although information was added as necessary to the computer record, early interpretative comments were never removed, only updated, as it was thought important to maintain as full a record as possible.

Very little manual planning was undertaken on site. Those areas planned by hand were drawn at 1:20 and tied in with the overall site survey. Sections were drawn at 1:10. All features were located using a Carl Zeiss ELTA 3 total station in conjunction with a Husky datalogger. The raw data was processed using Microsurveyor software and plans were generated using the Fastcad Computer Aided Design Package. Monochrome prints and colour slides were taken in 35mm format.

There were surprisingly few finds, especially in view of the heavily waterlogged nature of the site. A strategy of total collection for all classes of material was adopted as most appropriate, and all finds were handled and processed in accordance with LUAU standard practice following current IFA guidelines.

CHAPTER 2
THE EXCAVATIONS

The window of opportunity within the development programme at Dowbridge Close was limited and therefore demolition work and archaeological excavation took place simultaneously. For this and other reasons, the site provided substantial challenges in terms of excavation. Standing buildings and, in places, heavy contamination by oil meant that on several occasions trenches could not be placed where they would best answer questions, but only where there was room for them. Similarly, widespread more recent disturbance had left the already fragmented archaeological deposits further disrupted, with complex stratigraphic relationships surviving, on the whole, only within cut features and not between them. Between the major features, even the large ditches, few layers survived to establish relationships (Plate 4).

The evidence accrued proved equally difficult to interpret. Four coherent groups of features could, however, be distinguished on reasonable archaeological grounds, although there is little to link some of the individual elements within these groups except for their alignments and morphological similarities (Fig 3). They appear to manifest a broad chronological progression (Phases 1 to 4), although the high degree of residuality on the site (again the result of disturbance) has made them difficult to date, and it is quite likely that Phases 1, 2 and 3, whilst consecutive in the area of the fort, are partly or wholly indistinguishable elsewhere.

Phase 1, the earliest occupation of the site, proved the most difficult to define and is, rather, more a period during which several very short-lived events occurred (construction, use, and abandonment of the three possible temporary camps (Phases 1.2 to 1.4)). None of the sub-phases can be dated with accuracy but there is nothing to suggest that any of them are earlier than the Agricolan advance in the late AD 70s. Subsequently, parts of the site seem to have been extensively levelled (Phase 1.5) around the end of the first century AD, presumably as a preparation for the more permanent structures of Phase 2. Elsewhere, however, cut features (largely Phase 1.2, possibly towards the outside edge of the site as it then was) continued slowly to accumulate waste and debris well into the early decades of the second century AD, leading to severe problems with residuality. The lack of stratigraphic links has made it difficult to distinguish chronologically between Phases 1 and 2 and, whilst the Phase 2 signal station/fortlet seems likely to have replaced at least the earliest camp, others may have been in use simultaneously.

Dating as ever proved difficult, but it is likely that the Phase 2 activity may have been restricted to the late first century AD. The defensive ditches of the signal station/fortlet allow finer definition of the relative chronology within the phase as they were both re-cut and replaced (Phases 2.2, 2.3) before the entire installation was subsumed within a much larger and more standard fort (Phase 3.1) around the end of the first, or the early years of the second, century AD. Again the defences of this fort were refurbished and re-cut on two occasions (Phases 3.2, 3.3) before the fort was abandoned and allowed to fall into decay around the mid-second century AD.

Inevitably, a scatter of ill-defined, but possibly civilian, buildings grew up outside the successive military installations. These seem unlikely to have been domestic accommodation and may have been linked with industrial activity intended to service the needs of the fort. In this area the archaeological remains were particularly fragmented and it proved impossible to establish any significant divisions between events, except that the activity post-dated Phase 1. In consequence this has been discussed as Phase 2/3.

7

Following this there was little activity on the site. Disjointed and badly damaged features have been interpreted as medieval or later (Phase 4). In all probability they represent agriculture and stone robbing.

This report is presented in phase order, with each phase preceded by a brief introduction. The sub-phases are discussed individually and, within them, significant archaeological groupings are described separately. Palaeoenvironmental evidence has been incorporated within the main stratigraphic narrative and a summary of relevant finds evidence is presented at the end of each phase. Finally, the evidence from each phase is drawn together in a brief discussion.

The fragmented nature of the excavation has led to some features, especially the major ditches, appearing within several separate trenches and, in consequence, being allotted a number of context numbers. All relevant context numbers are listed in italics at the beginning of each sub-phase and the principal identifier for such features appears in boldface. This number alone appears within the written description.

Organisation of Volume

The main stratigraphic text is the joint work of Christine Howard-Davis and Kath Buxton, but has incorporated, where relevant, information provided by other contributors, particularly in relation to finds and palaeoenvironmental data. Unless otherwise stated, the finds reports are by Christine Howard-Davis; otherwise, individual contributors are credited for finds reports and catalogues in the relevant place. Ben Edwards provided much of the information on previous research and excavation in the vicinity. Only the main features for each phase are depicted on the figures, to give an overall view of the plan of the site.

CHAPTER 3
PHASE 1: THE EARLIEST ROMAN DEFENCES

The earliest features in the north-eastern part of the site (Trenches A and D), clearly preceded the first significant Roman activity. Although it is possible that they are prehistoric or Roman in date, they are rather more likely to be the result of natural process. The recovery from early features of several fragments of hand-made pottery, possibly of Iron Age type, might suggest a native presence, albeit slight, before or during the Roman period. The evidence is, however, insufficient to suggest that the site was ever formally occupied before the construction of the first Roman camp.

Phase 1 proper is represented by features associated with the construction and use of three substantial parallel military-type ditches of Roman date, each running approximately east to west across the eastern half of the site (Fig 4); it must be emphasised that they are not alike and may well have been associated with different temporary enclosures or forts. It would appear that the individual ditches were short-lived and, indeed, they may represent little more than a series of temporary camps.

The southernmost ditch (052) appears to have had a fairly brief life and to have been deliberately backfilled. The other two (006 and 056) seem to have silted up more slowly and both were subsequently re-cut in order to prolong their existence. Phase 1 proved difficult to date but it is presumed to have been relatively long, from the first inception of the military complex in the AD 70s, perhaps in the Governorship of Agricola, if not earlier, and possibly throughout Phase 2, until the early second century when any temporary fortifications were superseded by a substantial stone-built fort complex (Phase 3).

Phase 1.1: The Earliest Activity

Subsoils
Contexts 116/066/067/068/069/298/498/499
Natural subsoils (116), either buff to reddish orange clays or yellow sand, were encountered in all the trenches excavated and the great majority of archaeological remains were cut into, or lay directly above, them.

Small features
Contexts 015, 016, 017, 042, 043, 060, 061, 062, 063, 064, 065, 081, 082, 083, 084, 102, 103
A few features on the site appeared to predate the first significant Roman activity (Phase 1.2). There is, however, little to suggest that they were anything other than natural or short-lived, since they were isolated and undated.

Two narrow, irregular linear slots were identified in the east of the site (Trench A). One, 064 (0.70m wide and 0.20m deep), was filled with greyish white silty clay 065, and the other, 060, aligned north-south and only 0.18m wide, had a similar clay fill (061). It was deeper than 064, at 0.30m, but neither the full depth nor the profile could be determined. A third linear feature (062) cut 060 and was again filled by a mottled, re-deposited natural clay (063). Another group, of three features (Trench A), was covered by, and thus earlier than, the upcast from ditch 052 (012, Phase 1.2). One, an amorphous hollow (042) *c* 2.00m in diameter but only 0.05m deep, was filled with greyish brown silty clay (043). The other two, linear slots 081 and 083, were almost identical. Both were 0.60m to 0.70m long with U-shaped profiles around 0.20m deep, and ran east-west. Their fills, too, were alike, mid-grey silty clays containing a few charcoal fragments and stones (082, 084). As the slots were separated only by a slight ridge of clay, it seems probable that they were, in fact, parts of a single larger feature. Although the upper parts of fills 061 and 063 contained Romano-British tile and pottery, the amorphous form of all features strongly suggested that they were the result of tree root or animal disturbance.

Two more features in Trench A could be assigned to this phase. Feature 102 was a curving slot, 0.48m wide and 0.28m deep, with relatively steeply sloping sides and a narrow, flat base. The fill (103) was a mixture of reddish and buff grey sandy clays. Pit 015 was lozenge-shaped in plan, approximately 1.10m long, 0.68m wide, and 0.30m deep, with steeply sloping sides and a rounded bottom. The earliest fill (017), 0.10m of dark greyish brown sandy loam with a few stones and charcoal flecks, was sealed by 016, 0.20m of pinkish red clay. Both features were cut by a later ditch (004, Phase 1.3).

Hollow (or ditch) 135
Contexts 135/205, 137, 196, 197, 200, 201/259, 202, 206, 208, 209, 256, 257, 258
Feature 135, a substantial hollow or possibly a ditch (its full extent could not be determined), lay to the south of the early ditches (Trench D). The main part of this feature clearly ran north-south but there may also have been an east-west return (badly obscured by later activity and staining from spilt heating oil). Hollow 135 was up to 5m wide with a rather unusual profile, some 2m deep, with steep sides and a very flat bottom. The primary fill (201) was a light grey silty clay incorporating charcoal, covered by a series of mid grey silty clay layers (196, 200, 209, 257), interleaved with brownish orange clays (137, 206, 256, 258). The latest fills (197, 202) were both rather more sandy and incorporated a few cobbles (208). Although it can be suggested that this feature might be natural in origin, wide flat-bottomed ditches are not unknown in Roman defensive systems (Edwards *et al* 1985) and the relatively large (in comparison with the site as a whole) collection of finds from the upper fills suggests that it was a man-made feature. It obviously predates the first of the more typical defensive military ditches (052, Phase 1.2), having been cut by it, and may represent the earliest certain Roman activity on the site.

Phase 1.2: The First Temporary Camp

Ditch 052
Contexts 012, 052/195/254, 053, 108, 109, 110, 111, 112, 113, 114, 115, 136/255, 198, 199
Ditch 052 appeared stratigraphically to be the earliest of the three major Phase 1 ditches excavated (052, 006, 056; Fig 4). It ran east-west across the southern part of the site (Trench A) for some 61.5m before turning northwards, suggesting a western return (Trench D). It had been cut with the steep V-shaped profile often associated with Roman military ditches although, roughly 0.60m from the base, the angle of the sides became gradually gentler. It varied between 0.68m and 1.30m in depth (at the shallowest point (Trench D) it had obviously been badly truncated by later activity). The southern arm of the ditch was some 2.30m wide, increasing to 3.80m across the south-western corner.

The earliest fills appear to have accumulated naturally within the ditch, possibly in rather wet conditions. In the southern arm (Trench A), the thin layer of primary silt (115, light grey silty clay) was covered by 114, 0.10m of mixed, slightly sandy silty clay, and 113, a second thin layer of silt. The later fills, in contrast, were mainly redeposited natural clays (053, 109, 110, 112) interspersed with lighter grey silty clays (108, 111), which together formed a thick deposit (012) of what appeared to be the original upcast spoil from the ditch apparently deliberately pushed back in, presumably to level it. Fills from the western return echoed the above sequence (brownish orange clay 198, grey silty clay 199, and grey brown silty clay 136). Few finds were retrieved from this ditch, possibly implying that it was backfilled quite soon after it had begun to silt up and thus was quite short-lived.

A possible palisade or revetment
*Contexts **023**, 024, 032, 037, 038*
A second, less substantial, linear feature (023) lay directly north of, and parallel to, ditch 052 (Trench A). Although there was no direct stratigraphic link between the two, their close alignment suggests that they might have been contemporary. The full length of 023 could not be established, but it was 1.40m wide and 0.40m deep, with steeply sloping sides which opened slightly towards the top. The lower fill (024) consisted of grey silt with a charcoal fleck, incorporating loose clods of natural clay. Its mixed nature and the redeposited clay again suggested rapid and deliberate backfill. The upper fill (032) comprised *c* 50% rounded cobbles in a slightly darker silty matrix, which similarly implied a deliberate deposit rather than a randomly accumulated fill, as the natural subsoils were not particularly stony.

Feature 037 (0.30m wide and 0.10m deep) ran parallel to the northern edge of 023. The marked similarity of its fill (038) to those of 023 implied that it was not in fact separate but represented differential filling of a single feature, perhaps on either side of a barrier, presumably a fairly simple vertical structure. It is suggested that together 023 and 037 in fact represent the foundation trench for a palisade or timber revetment running along the lip of the ditch, probably retaining an upcast bank, and forming a defensive barrier.

Other features
*Contexts 228, 229, **302**, 347, 348, 349, **363**, 364, 365*
There were no other features that could be closely associated with the southern ditch (052). Several could, however, be tentatively assigned to Phase 1.2 on the grounds that they appeared to be earlier than the second major ditch, 006 (Phase 1.3 below).

An amorphous hollow, 363, appeared to an early feature in the southern part of the site (Trench H). It was about 0.76m in diameter and 0.32m deep, with two fills: 365, a light grey silty clay, and 364, a dark grey clayey silt. It was cut by ditch 302, some 2.50m wide, with a V-shaped profile *c* 1.00m deep, which ran approximately north-south through the area. This ditch contained three fills: grey silty clays 347 and 349, and brownish orange clay 348. Its purpose was not evident but since it lay at right angles to ditch 052 (although there was no direct stratigraphic link) it seems reasonable to suggest that it formed part of the same system.

Another small ditch (228, 2.50m wide, up to 0.25m deep, with a U-shaped profile) lay some 10m to the west of 302 (also in Trench H). It was filled by a silty clay loam (229) which varied from dark yellowish brown to dark greyish brown in colour. The fill was unusual in that it produced a relatively large number of finds, including burnt bone and charcoal, perhaps suggesting the disposal of domestic waste. It ran east-west but curved north at its eastern end and did not link with ditch 302.

Phase 1.3: The Second Temporary Camp

Ditch 006
*Contexts **006**/224/308/336, 007/059, 090, 091, 098, 099, 100, 101, 225, 226, 227, 230, 281, 282, 283, 313, 314, 315, 337, 338, 339, 342*
Ditch 006 lay at an angle to ditch 052, between 4.1m and 10.7m to the north. It, too, had a V-shaped profile, but varied substantially in width over a relatively short distance, from 1.30m (Trench A) to over 3.00m (Trench K). The depth also changed, though less drastically, from 0.90m to *c* 1.20m, perhaps reflecting truncation of the stratigraphy (levelling?) at an early date.

A similar stretch of ditch to the west (Trench E/H: 224, 336), and on the same line as 006, has been interpreted as part of the same defensive circuit. Ultimately it turned north forming a western return (Trench L). There appeared, however, to be a break in the line of this ditch as no trace of it was encountered in sections cut across a line projected between the two excavated segments (Trenches K and W). Such a break is likely to represent an entrance, but other explanations, such as later truncation or a turn, cannot be entirely ruled out. The junction between ditch segments 224 and 336, presumably a south-western corner, was not identified but again, their marked similarity and the certainty that 224 did not continue westwards beyond the line of 336 (Trench L) strongly suggested that they were part of the same circuit.

The number of fills varied between three (Trench K: 313, 314, 315) and seven (Trench E/H: 225, 226, 227, 230, 281, 282, 283). Fills in the western arm of this ditch (Trench L: 337, 338, 339, 342) appeared somewhat more organic in content and were partly waterlogged. Fills in the southern arm (Trench A: 007, 090, 091, 098, 099, 100, 101) were also somewhat organic in nature, and five of them had obviously been deposited from the north side of the ditch. They comprised layers and lenses of sandy clay loam varying in colour from yellowish brown to orange brown and grey.

Palaeoenvironmental evidence suggests that the ditch fills varied considerably in content, presumably indicating the deposition of material by different methods and from a number of sources. The sandier fills (eg 339, sample 1248) gave little indication that they had ever contained organic material, whilst the clays (eg 227, sample 1111) produced only small assemblages of plant remains, most of them weeds, and a few invertebrates of little consequence. The more organic fills (eg 338, sample 124703) were rich in very well-preserved plant remains, especially weeds and grassland plants. Amongst the former, there were large numbers of seeds or fruits of black nightshade, two *Chenopodium* species (fat-hen and fig-leafed goosefoot) and persicaria. All of these plants are likely to be abundant on dung-heaps or similarly eutrophic substrates. The grassland suite may well have included plants from hay, perhaps arriving in manure, but there was also a cereal component in the form of 'bran' and traces of uncharred ?wheat chaff. 'Straw' fragments in moderate amounts, sometimes in small clumps, suggest that cut vegetation, hay and/or straw, was also incorporated in the fills. The presence of two salt-marsh plants, *Triglochin maritima* and *Juncus gerardi*, is consistent with hay from, or dung from animals grazing on, salt-marsh meadows; such pastures were presumably available quite close to the site, for example on the Ribble estuary, today about 5km to the south, if not rather nearer (both plants have been recorded in the area in recent decades, *cf* Perring and Walters 1962).

The insect remains suggest the deposition of fresh dung, since there were grain pests, an appreciable component of foul decomposers, and a small number of species likely to have originated within buildings. There was, however, no well-developed community to indicate accumulated heaps of dung, or stable manure as such, and the records of seven *Aphodius prodromus* and three *A granarius* might indicate dung deposited by animals which were simply pastured close to the ditch. The numerous insect taxa likely to have originated in weedy waste ground reinforce this interpretation. The single human flea, *Pulex irritans*, had no obvious entry route but this species would probably be able to pass its larval stage in stable litter and might, therefore, have been dumped in stable manure or (like any of the 'indoor' species) have been accidentally eaten in fodder from the stable floor and subsequently voided in the open.

Aquatic insects were a little more abundant than would seem likely in the absence of at least temporary standing water, and there were small numbers of water flea resting eggs. No truly aquatic plant taxa were recorded; the few wetland forms may have been part of the hay/grazing component or may have simply lived on soils with impeded drainage close to the site of deposition.

In summary, evidence suggests that this ditch occasionally contained open water in small amounts and was accumulating plant and invertebrate remains from its wider environs, an area with quite substantial amounts of dung. This perhaps leads to speculation that livestock (probably horses) were kept or pastured in the immediate vicinity. Evidence at Ribchester (Buxton and Howard-Davis forthcoming) has established that there, at least, considerable numbers of horses, probably cavalry mounts, appear to have been periodically corralled immediately outside the fort.

Re-cut 129
Contexts **080, 129/316, 309, 310, 311, 312**
Towards the eastern end of the ditch (Trenches A and K) the upper fills (007, 315) may have been disturbed by a partial re-cut (129). The fills within this varied. Only one (080, mottled, redeposited clay) was noted to the east (Trench A), whilst in contrast, further west (Trench K) there were four (309, 310, 311, 312). These appeared to be rather more mixed than 080, although they were still mainly redeposited clays with lenses of grey silty clay and a deposit of cobbles (309).

Subsidiary ditch 004
Contexts **004**, *005/093*
Another less substantial ditch (004) ran north-south across the eastern end of the site (Trench A), effectively at right-angles to the large defensive ditches (052, 006, 056). It was significantly shallower than any of the others (only 0.75m deep) and contained a single, homogeneous mid-grey silty clay fill (005). Ditch 004 clearly cut the fills of the southern ditch (052) but its relationship with the central ditch (006 and re-cut 129) could not be satisfactorily defined. There was no doubt that they intersected, more or less at 90º, but it was not possible to determine whether ditch 004 cut ditch 006 alone, or both ditch 006 and re-cut 129. It is suggested, however, that ditch 004 may have been contemporary with the re-cut (129), thus allowing pit 015 and linear feature 102 (*see* page 10) to be assigned to Phase 1.1.

Phase 1.4: The Third Temporary Camp

Ditch 056
Contexts **056/304/425**, *070, 071, 079, 088, 089, 159, 160, 161, 162, 163, 164, 165, 166, 305, 469, 471, 472, 473, 474, 475, 476*
The most northerly, and probably the latest, of the three defensive ditches, 056 (Plate 5), lay *c* 8.10m to the north of ditch 006 (Trenches A, J and K). It was similar in size to the southernmost ditch (052, Phase 1.2), at 2.50m to 2.70m wide and up to 1.25m deep, but had a markedly different profile. Although on the same alignment, the westernmost part of the ditch (Trench N: 425) was significantly shallower (only 0.50m) which raised the possibility that this feature was not, in fact, a continuation of ditch 056, but a separate feature (Plate 6); were this the case, then ditch 056 must have ended or turned before reaching this point. Where excavated, the southern side of the ditch was almost vertical (70º or more), whilst the northern side was closer to 45º. Such an asymmetrical profile is typical of the so-called Punic ditch and can be paralleled at the neighbouring fort of Ribchester, where it appears to have been used to delimit a temporary fort boundary during a period of rebuilding (Buxton and Howard-Davis forthcoming, Phase 3). Webster (1979, 169) associates this type of ditch with temporary defences, which would not be inappropriate here, or places them ditches at the outside edge of defensive systems (*op cit*, 175).

Most of the fills in ditch 056 appeared to have been deposited as a series of small, separate dumps; 'tip lines' suggested that the bulk of the material was deposited from the south. There was a significantly greater number of fills (13 in Trench A, seven in Trench N), and a greater variety of material deposited in this ditch, than in either of the earlier defensive ditches. This perhaps suggests that it might well have been used over an extended period for waste disposal and thus have remained open somewhat longer than its predecessors. The majority of fills (Trench A) were 0.15-0.20m thick, although thinner lenses were observed (071, 089, 163) and the two latest deposits, 011 and 057, were thicker. In addition to the very dark brownish black silty clay primary deposit (166), four types of fill were noted: orangish brown redeposited natural, often with grey clay inclusions (071, 089, 161, 164), blue grey plastic clay (088 and 165), brown, gritty silty clay (159, 160, 079), and smoother material (070, 162, 163 and 166). Most fills in the western section (Trench N: 469, 471, 473, 474, 475, 476) were very similar to those already listed, but there was in addition a thick layer (0.30m) of very organic blackish silt (472). Traces of charcoal, industrial residues and burnt bone in the latest fills imply the disposal of waste.

Fill 088 (Trench A, sample 1016) contained little of palaeoenvironmental significance: a few poorly preserved plant macrofossils, including seeds of the toad-rush (*Juncus bufonius*), along with some other, tentatively identified, *Juncus* spp, which are likely to have grown on soils with impeded drainage, a track, path, or perhaps the bottom of a ditch in which water accumulated from time to time. No invertebrate remains were found and it is conceivable that this fill was, in fact, redeposited surface material.

The small residue from fill 425 (Trench N, sample 1251) consisted mainly of herbaceous plant detritus although 'seeds' were present in moderate numbers and were well preserved. The two groups most abundantly represented were weeds of waste and cultivated ground (including taxa of cereal fields) and plants of grassland habitats. There were also moderate amounts of wheat/rye 'bran' fragments, presumably originating from grain or flour. The most abundant beetles, *Oryzaephilus surinamensis* and *Cryptolestes ferrugineus*, are both pests of stored products, particularly grain; the presence of a single grain weevil confirmed the latter. The close association of evidence for cereals with the remains of grassland plants suggests that this deposit may have included either stable manure or dung from adjacent ground surfaces. The rarity of decomposer insects (other than a few fly puparia) was notable, although their diversity was high, indicating a mixed, probably random, origin. Thus, if stable manure was present, there had been no opportunity for the development of an insect fauna. The whole assemblage of beetles and bugs was of high diversity and had a substantial 'outdoor' component (itself of high diversity - a strong indication of the presence of a large proportion of 'background fauna').

The presence of numerous resting eggs (ephippia) of at least two species of water flea, one of them a *Daphnia* species, strongly indicates that ditch 056 held water, at least when fill 425 was deposited. Water beetles were a little more abundant than might be expected if there had been no water at all, but not enough to give evidence of permanent standing water. Although there were a few possible waterside/damp ground plant taxa, submerged and floating aquatic plants were absent and the combination of abundant water flea resting eggs with meagre aquatic plants and insects, seen frequently in archaeological ditch fills (H Kenward, pers comm), is interpreted as evidence of occasional standing water. Apart from the grain pests, the beetles and bugs almost certainly represent 'background fauna'.

Two very poorly preserved eggs of *Trichuris* sp were noted. It is impossible to determine whether these were human whipworm or one of the several species infecting other mammals including rodents, dogs, and foxes. The presence of eggs in such small numbers cannot be regarded as evidence of primary deposition of human faeces, especially in the absence of a full suite of remains of human foods.

Possible re-cut 553
Contexts 011, 057, 553
Examination suggested that 553, a linear feature, pit or gully, may have been cut through the upper layers of ditch 056 (Trench A: 159, 160) before it was finally filled. Its contents (011, 057) fitted well into the general range of material within the ditch. Whilst its full extent remains unknown, this was, however, so shallow (only 0.35m) and narrow (0.75m) that it seems unlikely to have been a systematic attempt to clear or renew the ditch, perhaps representing a smaller drainage gully. Post-medieval finds from the final fill imply some late disturbance of this feature.

Internal features
Contexts 369, 392, 393, 394, 395, 396, 397, 398, 399, 400, 401, 434, 435, 422/436, 437, 438, 439, 458, 462, 463, 483, 493
Several other features (Trench N) probably associated with Phase 1 were recorded within the circuit of ditch 056. There was little stratigraphic evidence to associate them directly with the defensive ditches, but all lay beneath clay layers which have been interpreted as debris deriving from the clearance of Phase 1 structures (Phase 1.5), probably levelling associated with construction during Phases 2 and 3; all have, therefore, been allocated to Phase 1.4.

Four pits were examined: 434, a small (1.1m by 0.75m) oval pit, was 0.22m deep, with gently sloping sides and a flat bottom. It was filled by 435, a greyish orange sandy clay. Pit 436 was *c* 1.5m in diameter and 0.35m deep with a fill, 437, very similar to 435. The largest of the pits, 458, was irregular in plan and the profile shelved shallowly to the east. It was some 2m across and 0.60m deep, with a flat base, and contained a sequence of three fills. The earliest (483) was a lens of black organic material, possibly decayed vegetation from the surrounding area. It was covered in turn by a similar depth of redeposited natural clay (463) and a uniform dark brown silty clay (462). The fourth pit, 369, lay to the north of the other three, partially beneath the eastern baulk of the excavation. The sides were vertical with little erosion or slumping, and the base flat except for a circular posthole in the north-west corner. Only 0.25m in diameter and 0.30m deep, this was filled by 439, a mix of redeposited natural clay, grey sandy silt and organic material. The vertical sides may suggest that the pit had originally been lined or, alternatively, that it had been backfilled very swiftly after it was dug. The organic nature of the fills suggests that it was probably a cesspit/latrine and thus perhaps plank-lined; the single posthole was possibly the remnant of a covering structure or internal seating. The fills comprised decayed sandstone (401) and pungent, grey or brownish black organic silty clays (393, 396, 397, 398) interspersed with the usual layers of orangish brown redeposited natural (392, 393, 394, 399) and layers made up of a mix of the two (395, 400, 438).

Phase 1.5: Clearance and Levelling

Contexts 386/464, 387, 388, 465/466, 467, 468, 470, 494
All four pits (Phase 1.4) were overlain by layers of redeposited natural (388, 468, 494) between 0.03m and 0.15m thick, and grey silty clays (465, 467, 470), up to 0.35m thick, separated by a thin (0.07m) lens of distinctive light greyish-white clay (386), and 0.08m of charcoal and blackened wood (387). The latter perhaps implies clearance of debris from the site, at least in part by burning.

15

Finds

Hand-made pottery
Several vessel fragments in an undecorated, hard-fired, hand-made fabric (Fabric 4) were recovered from ditch 056 (Phase 1:4). Iron Age material is not known from either the Fylde or most of central and northern Lancashire, although it is known from further south at Castle Steads, Bury (M Fletcher, pers comm). The presence of such material in a Phase 1 context might suggest some early interaction with the local native population but is not sufficient to suggest any permanent Iron Age settlement on the hilltop.

Samian
Phase 1 produced 62 sherds of samian, 39% of the total assemblage, of which around 50% came from Phase 1.4. Of the ten sherds from Phase 1.1, nine date to the Hadrianic or early Antonine period, making this collection untypical of Phase 1 in general. The mean sherd weight of 14g is quite large and may indicate that the material has not been subject to much redeposition and movement. However, although there may have been little movement after deposition, the general dating of Phase 1 to the first and perhaps early second centuries must suggest much of this material was deposited some time after individual features had gone out of use.

The 12 sherds from Phase 1.2 contexts include a Dr 29 bowl dating to *c* AD 75-85 and two other Flavian fragments. In general, this material is earlier than that from Phase 1.1 and all but two sherds are pre-Hadrianic in date. Two sherds (136/1121, 115g and 229/1169, 55g) weigh considerably more than the site average (only *c* 6% of sherds from the total assemblage weigh more than 50g), but if they are excluded, the mean weight of the remaining assemblage is *c* 5.5g, considerably lower than that of the Phase 1.1 material.

Phase 1.3 produced seven sherds of samian, four of which date to the first century, and again include a Dr 29 fragment. Approximately 20% (29 sherds) of the samian from the site came from Phase 1.4. The period of use of the final complex may have been fairly short and, it is suggested, can be placed before the end of the reign of Trajan. Seventeen fragments are either Flavian or Flavian/Trajanic, with a general decline in the number of pieces dated towards the end of this period (AD 117). A further four very small fragments derived from Phase 1.5. There is, however, also a small assemblage of eight Hadrianic/Antonine pieces, perhaps marking the (possibly short-lived) period of demolition or levelling of dilapidated and/or abandoned structures prior to rebuilding.

One of the two stamped vessels, a Dr15/17 or 18 platter, came from ditch fill 088 (Phase 1.4). Unfortunately the stamp was extremely worn (Stamp 2).

Coarsewares
Phase 1.1 contexts produced 39 sherds of coarseware vessels, four of amphorae, and six of mortaria, which together represent 7% of the stratified material from the site. Linear features 060 and 062 (fills 061 and 063 respectively) produced a total of 16 sherds of rustic ware (Fabric 7), all from the same vessel, and dated to *c* AD 80-130. Sherds of a cooking pot and dish in Black Burnished Ware 1 (Fabric 1) came from the upper levels of hollow 135 (fill 209), indicating that the hollow must have lain open for some time, well into the AD 120s, possibly accumulating debris throughout the life of the site, and other vessels of second century date (eg Fig 10.1, a Wilderspool product) from the phase seem to confirm such an extended period. All the amphora are of South Spanish olive oil vessels (Fabric 20), a common type for this period, and all the mortaria seem likely to have originated from Wilderspool (Fabrics 30, 36).

There was a much larger group of material from Phase 1.2, some 56 sherds of coarsewares, 46 of amphorae, and three of mortaria, in total 14% of the stratified pottery from the site. Black Burnished Ware 1 was present in fills from both the ditch and the suggested palisade (fills 136 and 024 respectively); the forms present suggest a second century date. Other vessels from the palisade trench (fill 024) include a flagon in Fabric 5 (Fig 10.2) of late first to early second century date.

Most of the pottery (72%) was recovered from 229, the fill of a subsidiary ditch, which was possibly used for the disposal of domestic waste. Vessels included a lid (Gillam 1970, 339), dated to the late first/first half of the second century, as well as 38 sherds of South Spanish olive oil amphora (Fabric 20). Three sherds of a single mortarium (Fig 10.3), again a Wilderspool product were also recovered.

Some 7% of the stratified pottery derived from Phase 1.3: 32 sherds of coarsewares, 13 of amphorae, and three of mortaria. Black Burnished Ware (Fabric 1) was present in two of the fills of ditch 052 (007, 230) and the subsequent re-cut (fill 080), again suggesting a *terminus ante quem* in the early second century. Fill 230 also produced a Wilderspool mortarium fragment (Fig 10.5) likely to be Hadrianic in date, whilst a sherd of mortarium from the Verulamium region (Fabric 32) was noted in fill 226; Verulamium supplied mortaria to the North in the later first century AD. A fourth fill of 052 (338) produced a greyware jar (Fabric 11, Fig 10.4) of late first/early second century date as well as a South Spanish amphora handle (Fabric 20). A Wilderspool mortarium fragment (Fig 10.6) was also recovered from 005, the fill of the subsidiary north-south ditch (004), confirming the broad contemporaneity of the two features.

Phase 1.4 produced the largest group of material: 136 sherds of coarsewares, 52 of amphorae, and nine of mortaria, 27% of the stratified pottery, and is the largest group from the site. Material from drainage gully 553 (fills 011, 057), cut into ditch 056, included Black Burnished Ware, amongst which was a dish of early/mid second century date (Fig 10.7). Greyware vessels (Fabric 11) came from a number of ditch fills and included jars (Figs 10.9 and 10.10) and a dish (Fig 10.11), all of later first or second century date. Vessels in oxidised wares (Fabric 12) included flagons with either a single handle (Fig 10.12) or two (Fig 10.13), all of which date to the late first/early second century, and a dish (Fig 10.14), the form of which is paralleled at Ribchester in a Hadrianic context (Hird forthcoming a). Amphora fragments include vessels of South Spanish (Fabrics 20, 23) and Gaulish (Fabrics 21, 25, 26, Fig 10.15) origin. Mortaria sherds from three unrecognised sources (Fabrics 33-35) are present, as well as Wilderspool products, including one (Fig 10.16) with an unusual rim form.

Post-Roman pottery
A single fragment of post-medieval pottery and a clay pipe stem fragment must suggest that 011, the upper fill of gully 553 (Phase 1.4), was subject to some late disturbance.

Other finds
Phase 1 produced few other finds. Where these could be identified they were of Roman date, but were otherwise undiagnostic. Only three fragmentary iron nails and a short twist of lead wire were recovered, the nails from fills 017 (pit 015, Phase 1.1) and 011 (gully 553, Phase 1.4), the lead from 088, a fill of ditch 056 (Phase 1.4). A single small fragment of leather came from a fill (338) of ditch 006 (Phase 1.3), apparently deriving from a piece of good quality leatherwork, probably something like a saddle. A second piece, from ditch 056 (fill 472, Phase 1.4) was sheet leather, with a seam at one edge.

Three fragments of glass (one vessel and two window) came from Phase 1.1 and a further eight (seven vessel, one window) from Phase 1.2. The vessel fragments (one from palisade trench 023 and six from ditch 228 (fill 229)) were all of first/second century date, and the matte-glossy window fragment from ditch 052 (fill 136) is typical of the same period. Phase 1.3 produced part of a small dark blue glass globular bead (ditch 006, fill 007), and Phase 1.4 produced a single vessel fragment (gully 553, fill 057); neither are closely dated.

A small amount of wood was recovered (seven fragments). Of that from Phase 1.3, one piece (ditch 006, fill 227) appears natural in origin: split and warped, the wood bears no toolmarks and is badly insect-damaged, although it may be partially burnt. Another small fragment from the same ditch (fill 339) was, however, clearly modified, part of a radially split plank with adze-dressed surfaces. Again partially burnt, it implies the use of substantial timbers. A single small charred fragment from Phase 1.4 (ditch 056, fill 472) was badly damaged. The presence of modified wood and evidence of burning perhaps suggests the use of scrap wood for fuel.

A fragment of vitrified hearth lining and 35 pieces of incidentally fired clay, possibly from a hearth or kiln superstructure, were recovered from ditch 228 (fill 229, Phase 1.2). Brick and heat-damaged thick tile fragments came from the same context. Although ditch 228 does not resemble a kiln or hearth in any way, the amount of industrial debris within it, along with charcoal and burnt bone, strongly suggests that it may, in part, have been filled with debris from such a structure. Small amounts of burnt clay, possibly associated with industrial processes, were recovered from a number of other contexts (005, 007, 088, 136, 164, 466). This can derive from a number of sources, such as clay hearths, kilns, or moulds, as well as from burnt wattle and daub structures, but amounts were too small to determine an origin. Apart from this material, tile and brick was also recovered from Phase 1.2 palisade trench 023 (fill 024) and ditch 052 (fill 111), Phase 1.3 ditch 006 (fills 080, 091) and Phase 1.4 ditch 056 (fills 070, 305). Drainage gully 553 (fills 011, 057, Phase 1.4), which cut ditch 056, also produced a little tile (roof and flue) and brick, as did destruction layer 466 (Phase 1.5). The presence of both roof and box tile might imply reasonably substantial buildings in the vicinity, although late disturbance (fill 011) means that such buildings may not necessarily have been associated with the early life of the complex.

Discussion

Phase 1 proved difficult both to excavate and to interpret, and the conclusions about the earliest Roman defences on the site are drawn from relatively scant evidence. It was often impossible to link sections of ditch across trenches and, when links were made, it seemed that ditches had changed markedly within relatively short distances (Plates 5 and 6). Other features were often stratigraphically isolated, or their relationships only sketchily determined, although a gross chronological sequence was established. The dating of the sub-phases remains to a degree problematic: all contained rather mixed groups of pottery (especially some of the Phase 1.1 features) which served only to confuse, rather than refine, the dating.

It is likely that some of the earliest features (Phase 1:1) are probably not man-made, while others containing pottery and charcoal may perhaps have been short-lived features associated with the first Roman occupation of the site. Several (eg hollow 135) present a problem, in that some of the pottery from the upper fills is contemporary with material from Phase 1.2, despite a clear stratigraphic relationship. The mixture can, perhaps, be accounted for in two ways: some of the smaller features appear to be natural in origin and later material may well have been carried down by tree root or animal action; or,

18

especially in the case of 135, they may have been slow to fill completely; as a large depression it may well have trapped later material.

Although it is not impossible that the three east-west ditches (006, 052 and 056) represent part of a fairly conventional defensive system of contemporary construction, several factors might suggest otherwise. It seems more likely that in fact they represent the close superimposition of at least two, possibly three, temporary camps and certainly this is implied by the position of the western returns of the first and second ditch circuits (052, 006). These seem to indicate overlapping single ditches rather than an integrated multi-ditch defensive system. The size of the ditches might suggest temporary camps, which conventionally had a single ditch 1m or so deep and around 2m wide, either V-shaped or Punic in profile, and any of the three would fit those requirements.

It seems likely from the layout of two of the three ditches (052 and 006), and the profile of the third (056), that the interiors of the camps always lay to the north, presumably pre-determining the position of the later, more permanent fort, although that lies slightly to the east, on the crest of the hill. There was no means of establishing a chronology between the three and dating from the ceramic assemblage proved inadequate but, since it clearly went out of use first and seems to have been deliberately backfilled before the end of Phase 1.2, it can be suggested that ditch 052 (Trenches A and D) and a revetted bank or palisade (023) represent the earliest camp.

It is perhaps impossible to separate ditches 006 (Trenches A, E/H, K and L) and 056 (Trenches A, J/N), but it must be noted that a Punic ditch like 056 was conventionally used alone (in a marching camp or in early defensive outworks) or as the outer line of a more complex defence, since it was intended to trap attackers within the field of fire (Webster 1979). Ditch 056 lies close to the edge of the excavated area (Trench A) and, if it were the outermost line in a more complex defensive system, any further ditches would lie beyond the excavations. Ditch 004 was aligned at right angles to the defensive ditches. Stratigraphically it appears to have been in existence, if not when the middle ditch (006) was in use, at least when its line was still obvious, and it is suggested the creation of 004 may have coincided with the partial renewal (129) of ditch 006. Thus it can be inferred that ditch 004 was linked in some way with the defences.

Few other features were linked with sub-phases 1.2 to 1.4. Investigation of the series of three small pits (434, 436, 458) offered little evidence as to their function, but a fourth (369) appears to have been a lined cesspit or latrine.

Finds do little to illustrate activity. Small amounts of iron nails, brick and tile, including roof tile (*tegula*) and box tile, imply some tile-roofed buildings and the presence of at least one hypocaust-heated building in the vicinity, although this material may well have been intrusive. Likewise, the presence of window glass confirms that there must have been reasonably substantial buildings in the area although the amount, a single fragment, is hardly indicative that these were associated with this phase of activity. Other finds were sparse and inconclusive.

The interpretation of several of the earliest features as the result of tree-root disturbance would concur with environmental evidence from elsewhere on the Fylde (Wells *et al* 1997) that morainal hummocks and ridges, such as that upon which the Roman fort was founded, were probably reasonably heavily wooded during most of the Iron Age and were not exploited, even for agriculture, until the late Iron Age/Romano-British period. It is suggested that the hilltop was not settled at the time when the Romans arrived, although a few fragments of hand-made pottery from a Roman context might suggest a native population in the vicinity. Dense woodland could have provided timber, felled and converted on the spot, for the construction of the first camps during a period of rapid advance, when it was highly unlikely that bulk construction materials would have been carried by, or have even followed closely behind, troops on campaign.

The pottery demonstrates clearly the amount of residuality encountered on the site. The absence of pre-Flavian forms amongst the samian, however, suggests that the military installation at Kirkham was probably not founded before the Agricolan advance in the late AD 70s, unlike its neighbours at Ribchester (Buxton and Howard-Davis forthcoming) and Lancaster (Jones and Shotter 1988), and further north at Carlisle (McCarthy 1993), which can all now be demonstrated to have been founded before that event. Shotter has speculated, by analogy with his later Scottish campaigns, that Agricola used troops and fleet *in tandem* and that 'it was Agricola's policy to disembark troops in the main estuaries and march them up the valleys where they could join with troops taking overland routes' (Shotter 1984, 7). He further suggests that the fort at Kirkham may have originated in such a fashion and it is tempting to see initial Roman occupation as a temporary camp founded by Agricola in the course of his campaign of conquest. Consideration of sea-level evidence suggests that Kirkham may well have been closer to a sea inlet at this time and it is possible to imagine the fort founded to guard a vital entrepot for both troops and supplies, the army then moving east to skirt the more-or-less impenetrable mosses of the Fylde, and ultimately north, via the fort at Ribchester (probably renovated at this time, see Buxton and Howard-Davis forthcoming). This first camp was without doubt short-lived and presumably abandoned or levelled as the first troops moved on, possibly later to be replaced at intervals by the second and third temporary camps.

It seems likely that Phases 1 and 2 overlap considerably and thus it might seem logical to suggest that the end of Phase 1 coincided with the rebuilding of the fort in stone around the middle of the second quarter of the second century. If, as at Ribchester, extant middens and accumulated rubbish were used to backfill open ditches, this would account in part for the high degree of residuality which appears to be associated with pottery which is not much abraded.

CHAPTER 4
PHASE 2: THE SIGNAL STATION/FORTLET

The dating of Phase 2 also proved extremely difficult and must remain somewhat fluid, based as often on assumption as on good stratigraphic relationships. There proved to be no direct stratigraphic link between any Phase 2 feature and the three large defensive ditches of Phase 1, although there were more obvious stratigraphic links between the features of Phases 2 and 3. In consequence, the features described below can only be said to be possibly, but not necessarily, later than those of Phase 1, but definitely earlier than the stone fort assigned to Phase 3, since the Phase 3 ramparts overlay some Phase 2 features. Phase 2 is deemed to cover the lifetime of a small military enclosure interpreted as a watch tower and/or fortlet (Fig 5).

Phase 2.1: The First Defences

Ditch 140
Contexts 140/231/543, 141, 142, 143, 144, 145, 146, 147, 148, 149, 150, 151, 152, 153, 154, 155, 156, 157, 232, 233, 234, 235
Ditch 140 was the earliest feature assigned to Phase 2. It is interpreted as representing the entire southern, and parts of the eastern and western, sides of a small defended enclosure (Trenches C, G and U respectively), possibly a signal station or fortlet, lying for the most part beneath the later fort (Phase 3). The ditch was relatively large, around 2.70m wide and 1.25m deep, with a typical military (Plate 7), V-shaped profile, tapering in to a narrow 'ankle breaker', only 0.20m wide, at the bottom. Towards the west (Trench U) ditch 140 appeared to be curving northwards, possibly forming a western return, suggesting a total length of 47.25m for the southern side of the enclosure. Although badly damaged at the corner by later features, the western arm of the enclosure ditch appeared to end shortly after the turn, presumably indicating the position of an entrance.

A section across the ditch (Trench C) revealed a succession of up to 17 fills. In general terms the fills were very similar, grey, highly organic, and friable. They could, however, be divided into two broad groups, thin lenses up to 0.08m deep (141-146, 150, 152, 153), and thicker layers, on average between 0.20m and 0.30m in depth (147-149, 151, 154-157). The majority were clays with either sandy or silty inclusions, in various shades of grey (142-144, 147-151, 153, 155, 156), interleaved with layers of more mixed material containing natural orange brown clay (146, 152, 157). Only three layers differed markedly: the primary silt, a thin layer of brown silty sand (141), 145, a thin layer of yellowish brown silty sand, and 154, a much thicker (0.25m) layer of cream-coloured clayey sand.

Palaeoenvironmental evidence from one of the grey clay layers (148, sample 1040) was meagre. A single weevil, *Otiorhynchus* sp, was the only recognisable insect, and the state of the assemblage was typical of a deposit from which the bulk of insect remains had completely decayed. A few poorly preserved plant macrofossils were also recorded. The most abundant were seeds of the rush *J bufonius* and, although in isolation they merely suggest land with impeded drainage, a trace presence of Greater Plantain seed could imply areas of trampled ground in the vicinity.

Many of the lower fills of ditch 140 were highly organic in content, suggesting that they accumulated in relatively wet, anaerobic conditions. They were also in places closely interleaved with natural subsoils slumped or redeposited from the edges of the ditch. It would thus seem likely that the enclosure ditch remained open and wet for some time, allowing its sides to weather and erode, gradually silting it up. There is some evidence (Trench G only) to suggest that the ditch

21

was modified in some way, possibly collapsed or partially backfilled, before later being re-cut, but this may well have been very localised, and perhaps only a temporary measure.

A second section across ditch 140 (Trench G: 231) revealed only four fills: the primary deposit (232), 0.10m of black organic silt, was covered by 233, a dark grey silty clay, and 234, a thin layer of organic material. Here, in contrast to the sequence described above, the upper part of the ditch was filled with a distinct layer of redeposited natural clay (235), perhaps implying a deliberate act of backfilling, and thereby possible reorganisation, although what, and at what scale, remains unclear. It also seemed that the ditch might subsequently have been re-cut (221) in this area, disturbing the upper fills (see Phase 2.2).

Internal features
*Contexts 118, 119, 120, 121, 122, 123, 124, 125, 126, 266, 267, **289**, 290, **291, 292, 293***
Only a small part of the internal area of the signal station/fortlet could be examined (Trenches C, G and U), and in places (eg Trench U) all potential evidence for internal features had been destroyed by later activity.

Four large postholes (289, 291, 292, 293) lay within the south-east corner of the enclosure (Trench G). Their layout and appearance suggests that they might have been part of a somewhat larger structure which lay wholly within the ditch circuit. The most southerly of those recorded, 291, lay directly under the rampart of the later fort, confidently establishing them as earlier than Phase 3.

The postholes were fairly uniform in appearance, roughly oval with the long axis around 1.30m long, and 289 proved to be 0.77m deep, with vertical sides and a flat base. It was filled with stiff orange clay (290), probably returned spoil from its original excavation. Forming a 'structure' approximately 4 x 3m, the postholes can most easily be interpreted as part of the foundations for either a signal tower or an internal barrier, like that in the fortlet at Rotelsee (Planck 1975), or internal buildings such as those at Martinhoe, Devon (Collingwood and Richmond 1976, 61), where an 80ft (24.4m) square enclosure is thought to have housed about a hundred men. A similar enclosure in Cumbria, Robin Hood's Butt (*op cit*, 63), contained a 20ft (6.1m) square stone tower overlooking the sea, and it seems clear that Burgh 1 on the Solway Firth incorporates a very similar structure (Daniels 1989, 23), as does Farnhill on the Solway (D Shotter, pers comm). Contemporary Scottish signal towers (Collingwood and Richmond 1976, 62-3) tended to be smaller (internally 30-40ft (9.1-12.2m) in diameter) and round, and often with only a single four-post structure.

The only other features which could be regarded as probably contemporary with this phase were a series of thirteen stakeholes (Trench C: 118, 119-126) and a single small posthole (Trench G: 267). Five of the shallow, circular stakeholes, all about 0.35m apart, formed a line (118) some 2m long, running roughly east-west. Although no firm identification can be made, it might be suggested that they represent a line of tent pegs. The remaining eight (119-126), however, were rather more randomly disposed. Posthole 267 was only 0.35m in diameter and 0.30m deep, filled with an orange brown sandy silt (266).

Phase 2.2: Modification of the Defences

Re-cut 221
*Contexts **221**, 222, 263, 264, 265*
Ditch 221 (Trench G) may well represent a partial re-cut or clearance of ditch 140. It was *c* 1.10m wide and 0.30m deep with a flat base and near vertical sides, and obviously respected the edges of its predecessor, strongly suggesting that, at least in part, the earlier ditch may still have been visible. There were two fills: a clayey black, organic material with charcoal (222), and a mid-grey silty clay (263)

containing small rounded stones. Little palaeoenvironmental evidence survived in 222 (sub-samples 111001 and 111002), although lumps of somewhat indurated material formed a large proportion of that examined. This may have been peat or humic soil which had been dried, perhaps baked, but not burnt, at some stage, and perhaps, along with the charcoal, derived from localised and not very intense burning.

A second possible ditch (265) lay immediately to the east of 221. Although slightly shallower, at around 0.20m, it had a similar profile and contained a comparable black organic deposit (264). Although no firm connection could be established between the two, apart from their similarity and close proximity, it seems reasonable to suggest that both may have been associated in some way with a modification of the defensive circuit of the signal station/fortlet.

Further modification, ditch 194
*Contexts 189, 190, 191, 192, 193, **194**/236/544, 237, 238, 239, 240, 260, 261*
Ditch 194 appears to have laid immediately outside the original defensive circuit (ditch 140, Phase 2.1), but whether the two existed simultaneously, or this was a replacement, could not be determined. It is, however, suggested, somewhat intuitively, that it was a later replacement. This second, much smaller ditch followed the same course as 140 but differed markedly in plan, having an abrupt right-angle at the south-west corner, rather than the broad curve of its predecessor. Its profile (Trench C), too, was significantly different. It was distinctly U-shaped, some 0.75m deep, with a flat bottom between 0.20m and 0.35m across. At the top it was between 0.70m and 1.90m wide, the great variation probably a result of later truncation. It seems likely that ditch 194 ended in approximately the same place as ditch 140, although no obvious terminus was identified and the area in which it would have laid was much disturbed.

Ditch 194 contained a series of grey or grey brown silty clay fills (Trench C: 189-193; Trench G: 237-240, 260, 261), all of which were fairly similar to those in ditch 140. Again, palaeoenvironmental investigation (fill 237, sample 1109) produced little of significance; toad rush and sedge (*Carex* sp) presumably echo the wet conditions of the primary ditch.

*Possible outwork (*titulus*) 513*
*Context **513**, 517, 518*
Another small ditch, 513 (Trench T), lay to the west of the two ditches which enclosed and defended the signal station/fortlet. Although it could not be related to the others stratigraphically, it lay on roughly the same alignment, suggesting a link. Also, the profile of ditch 513 closely resembled that of ditch 194, again implying that they may have been related (Plate 8).

Ditch 513 was around 1.20m wide and 1m deep, with an 'ankle breaker' bottom; it had a squared end to the east. There were only two fills, light grey silty clay 517 and dark grey friable silt 518, with patches of sand and a few fragments of wood. Given that it apparently lay across, and at some distance from, a possible entrance to the signal station/fortlet, it might be that it formed part of either a *titulus*-type entrance or some other defensive outwork, impeding access to the enclosure. *Tituli* often appear to be associated with temporary camps (Webster 1979, 171), but it could be suggested that if the signal station/fortlet was associated with the series of temporary camps assigned to Phase 1, some variation to the usual defensive system could be expected.

Other external features
Contexts *367, 368/389, 370,* 372, 373, 374, 375, 376, 377, 378, 379, 380, 381, 382, 383, 402, 403, 404, 405, *424, 457, 477, 478,* 479, 480, 481, 482, 484, 495

The destruction debris (Phase 1.5) which covered ditch 056 (Phase 1.4) was cut by 424, a large, flat bottomed pit *c* 2.40m in diameter, 1.15m deep, and containing a succession of five fills. The primary deposit was dark grey organic material 482, covered by brownish orange redeposited natural clay 481, dark grey silty clay 480, light grey sandy silt 479, and redeposited natural 495 which, as well as filling the upper part of the pit, overlay its edges. A second broadly similar feature (457) cut the fills of pit 424. As it ran beneath the eastern baulk of Trench N its shape and full dimensions could not be determined and it may either have been a pit or the rounded end of a ditch. It was at least *c* 2.10m wide and 0.40m deep, with a single grey silty clay fill, 484.

Both pits had been covered by two further layers of possible destruction or demolition debris. The earliest, 477, brownish orange re-deposited natural some 0.10m thick, was covered by a substantially thicker deposit (478), 0.40m of light grey silty clay.

The external features assigned to Phase 2.2 could not be placed within the chronological framework of the site with any precision, but all are without doubt stratigraphically later than Phase 1 and would most logically appear to predate the stone fort. It seems reasonable to suggest that large pits like 424 would not have been dug so close to the likely entrance of a Phase 3 annexe if it had already been in existence.

Three more intercutting pits (367, 368, 370), thought to be broadly contemporary with this phase, lay to the north of pits 424 and 457; all cut cesspit/latrine 369 (Phase 1.4 above).

Pit 368 was the earliest, roughly oval in plan (1.80m by 1.40m) and 0.46m deep, it was filled by grey silty clay (382), redeposited natural (380), and a mix of the two (379, 381, 383). The presence of a little worn *As* of Vespasian (AD 71) in fill 379 provides a *terminus post quem*. The second pit, 370, was round (2m diameter, 0.40m deep) with a flat but uneven base. To the east its sides were vertical but elsewhere, especially where it cut earlier ditch fills, they tended to be concave. It was filled by mottled orange and dark browny grey sandy silt (402) containing small stones and occasional charcoal flecks. A shallow depression (403) was noted within this fill, lying slightly off-centre to the west. It seems unlikely that this was deliberately cut and it probably represents a slight hiatus in the depositional succession, during which some subsidence or erosion might have taken place. Above it, fill 404 comprised a thin band of dark grey silty clay sandwiched between fine layers of pinkish yellow sand, covered in turn by mottled orange and browny grey silty clay 405.

The last pit in the sequence (367) cut both 368 and 369 (Phase 1:4). It was *c* 1m in diameter and tapered to a point in section. It contained seven fills which appeared to have either slumped or been thrown into the pit. The primary deposit (378) was 0.20m of pinkish sand with grey silty mottling, covered by a thin layer of dark grey, slightly silty clay (376), which incorporated a small patch of redeposited natural (377). Two further deposits of silty clay lay above 376. The first, 374, a mid-grey clay *c* 0.20m thick, included a thin lens of organic material and appeared to have entered the pit from the south. The second, 375, a mix of light grey and brownish orange clays, appeared to have been deposited from the north; a further 'lump' of redeposited natural (373) was incorporated in the upper part of this layer. The uppermost, and thickest (0.34m) fill was, again, a grey silty clay (372).

Finds

Very few finds were associated with this phase and so any attempt at dating, or explanation of activity, remains difficult.

Coarsewares
Sixteen sherds (2% of the stratified pottery from the site) of a single flagon in an oxidised ware (Fabric 12) were recovered from ditch 140 (fill 157, Phase 2.1). Phase 2.2 produced a total of 19 sherds of coarseware and one of amphora, approximately 3% of the stratified pottery. All were consistent with a late first/early second century date and included fragments of a second flagon in Fabric 12, a lid in Fabric 11, and a rusticated jar in Fabric 7.

Other finds
Although no industrial residues were recovered, small amounts of incidentally fired clay, possibly associated with industrial processes, were present in fill 157 (ditch 140, Phase 2.1) and within the fills of pit 370 (Phase 2.2). Likewise, a small amount of tile and brick was recovered from this pit but little can be inferred from its presence.

Discussion

Phase 2 has proved difficult to date, although stratigraphically it is without doubt earlier than the stone fort assigned to Phase 3, and possibly, though in much less clear-cut terms, subsequent to Phase 1. It is, however, likely that there was a considerable amount of overlap between the two earlier phases.

It has been suggested that Phase 1 represented the construction and use of a number of temporary camps, and it seems likely that the focus of activity characterised as Phase 2 lay outside these and may in fact have overlain at least one of them. If, as would appear possible from the lack of evidence, no full-sized timber fort was ever constructed on the site, then the Phase 2 defended enclosure may represent the only permanent Roman presence at this time, built at an occasional disembarkation point. In such a case the normal garrison was likely to have been very small.

Ditch 140, the most substantial feature assigned to this phase, appears to be the south side of a relatively small (c 60m across), probably square, defended enclosure. Within this enclosure a number of substantial postholes suggested a timber building(s) of considerable size. The enclosure was too small to have been even a modest fort and its shape, square with rounded corners, suggests a signal station or fortlet of some sort, perhaps similar to those known on the German Limes (Baatz 1975), and perhaps with several internal buildings rather than an isolated tower. Such an arrangement can be seen in the Neronian fortlet at Martinhoe, Devon (Collingwood and Richmond 1976, 61) and others of first and second century date. Such fortlets often seem to have been associated with coastal signalling, which could easily be the case at Kirkham if, as is suggested, it was effectively a haven at that time. In that case any tower would act as a beacon or lighthouse as well as signal relay.

Despite a lack of dating evidence, it seems that the signal station remained in use for some time and was eventually part-demolished, part-incorporated into the later fort, a situation perhaps paralleled at Bowness-on-Solway, where postholes beneath the later stone gateway were originally thought to be the remnant of an earlier timber gateway (Potter 1975, see especially 32). The original ditch appears to have silted up (or been in part backfilled) and re-cut, before being replaced by a second ditch immediately outside the line of the first. This ditch, 194, follows the line of the first but is markedly different in morphology, since rather than a typical, V-shaped profile and ankle breaker, it has a flat-bottomed,

U-shaped profile, perhaps suggesting that it was intended rather as the foundation trench for a substantial palisade than as a defensive ditch. The enceinte marked by this ditch, interestingly, has angular corners, rather than the curved corners of its predecessor, again implying that it was intended as support for a structure, perhaps a solid palisade, rather than as a defensive ditch.

A short length of ditch (513, recorded only in Trench T), lying parallel to, but to the west of, the line of ditches 140 and 194, and continuing the original line when they had both turned north, has been interpreted as possible evidence for a *titulus*-type defended entrance. It must be noted, however, that such complex entrances are most often associated with temporary camps (Webster 1979, 171) and not more permanent structures such as this signal station/fortlet appears to have been. Recently, however, evidence has been growing to suggest that numerous short lengths of ditch were on occasions dug at an angle to a more permanent military installation, presumably for extra defence (M Bishop, pers comm).

The installation was, in part, incorporated into the later stone fort and thus probably did not fall entirely out of use during the lifetime of its successor. The successive ditches were, however, allowed to fill, presumably as they became redundant to the defence of the fort.

Despite the substantial ditches, no evidence was found for an associated defensive bank. This may have been effectively cleared by the reconstruction of Phase 3 or may simply have never existed; and indeed it appears that many of the signal stations discussed by Collingwood and Richmond (1976) were not embanked, but the spoil from the ditches was spread over the surrounding area. Were this to be the case at Kirkham then it would be possible to see the clearance defined as Phase 1.5 as in fact the first act of Phase 2, allowing firmer stratigraphical definition between the two phases.

A small number of other features were regarded as contemporary with the signal station/fortlet, but rather on pragmatic grounds than on sound stratigraphic evidence. They were for the most part pits which appeared to lie across the entrance to a possible annexe east of the Phase 3 stone fort. Some of them were very large and since, if they were contemporary with the annexe this would have proved a somewhat inconvenient arrangement, blocking access, they are more sensibly regarded as either earlier or later than the stone fort; the former seems more likely.

CHAPTER 5
PHASE 3: THE FORT

Phase 3 is marked by the construction of a stone-revetted rampart, the circuit wall of a new and larger military installation (Fig 6). This was fronted with red sandstone which, although not local, could have been obtained easily from further east, probably around Preston, where it outcrops in a number of places. The rampart was defended by a substantial ditch, recut on two occasions. Evidence from the interior of the fort hinted at cobbled surfaces and buildings, although the latter lay so close to the modern ground surface that they were extensively disturbed and damaged by more recent activity. There was possibly an annexe to the east of the fort.

Phase 3.1: Construction and Early Use

Ditch 220 and outwork 538
*Contexts 219, **220**/322/408/456/546, 331, 332, 333, 409, 410, 490, 492, 538, 539, 540, 541, 542*
Ditch 220 provided defence for the southern (Trenches C, P and Q) and eastern (Trench G) sides of the new stone fort. Both the south-western and south-eastern corners of the defences were located, although the full extents of the western and eastern sides of the fort remain unknown. It is, however, likely that both ran north, eventually meeting with the ditches encountered by Pickering in the late 1950s and early 1960s (*see* Chapter 1, 3).

The full extent of the defences on the southern side of the fort was examined, some 124.20m in length. The south-east corner followed the line of the earlier (Phase 2) ditch system, but the new fort clearly enclosed a significantly larger area, running westwards beyond the early ditches to between two and three times the original length of ditch 140 (Phase 2.1). A break in the line, towards the centre of the southern side (Trench T), might suggest the position of an entrance, although there is no other firm evidence (the area was severely disturbed, and modern foundations limited the area available for excavation).

Ditch 220 had a surviving width of between 1.70m (Trench C) and 2.26m (Trench P) but, since the inner edge had been destroyed by two successive re-cuts (218 and 214), it was originally probably somewhat wider. Likewise the profile and depth varied, from sloping sides and a flattish base some 0.80m deep on the southern side, to V-shaped and around 0.70m deep on the east. Despite these differences, it is likely that the two excavated sections were part of the same circuit, and the changing profile reflects localised erosion or cleaning. The number and nature of fills in the southern arm of ditch 220 varied; at the eastern end three discrete fills were noted (Trench C: 333, 332, 331: all grey clays), but northwards there were only two (Trench P: 409, 410; Trench Q: 492, 490). In the eastern arm of ditch 220 (Trench G) only a single fill, 219, was present, closely resembling the primary fill (333, a plastic grey silty clay) encountered elsewhere (Trench C). The variety within the fills presumably represents a changing sequence of deposition along the length of the ditch.

A second ditch, 538 (Trench S), was recorded to the immediate west of the south-west corner of ditch 220. It was of similar dimensions (*c* 2.10m wide and 0.85m deep), with a gentle U-shaped profile. Although not stratigraphically linked to ditch 220 (other than by its relationship with topsoil), this ditch segment appeared to echo its line, running almost parallel, which, alongside evidence from the sequence of re-cuts (see 534, Phase 3.2, and 530, Phase 3.3), suggests that ditches 220 and 538 may have been contemporary.

The number of fills recorded in ditch 538 was greater than that of ditch 220. Ditch 538 was, however, cut into natural sand, and thus particularly susceptible to subsidence, which undoubtedly contributed to the increased number. The primary fill, 539, was a blackish sandy silt with patches of clean natural sand, which was covered in turn by 540, yellowish sandy clay, 541, grey clay incorporating at its base a thin band of peaty material, and 542, natural yellow sand, apparently redeposited. Only a short section of ditch was examined and thus its alignment is to some extent conjecture; further investigation, however, established its absence on the south side of the fort, indicating that, unlike 220, it did not provide a complete defensive circuit. It is therefore suggested that ditch 538 formed a defensive outwork (Wilson's group 2; Wilson 1984) intended to offer reinforcement at the western end of the fort.

Stone-fronted rampart
Contexts 075, 076/276, 077, 078/306/301, 117/288, 299, 300, 317, 318, 319, 320
The remains of what must have been a substantial stone-revetted rampart (Trenches C and G; Plate 9) lay within and parallel to the main defensive circuit (220). On the southern side of the fort, the line of the front of the rampart appears to have been fossilised as a property boundary, followed by the modern northern boundary of the area under examination. In consequence, the rampart proper lay beyond the confines of the site, but tumble from the revetment was recognised in several places (Trenches Q and T).

Only the very bottom of the earthen rampart survived (Trench C: 078) as a shallow ridge of turves, 3.50m to 4.50m across. Within this, small, distinct lenses of varying composition (black organic clay, brown, grey, or cream silty clays, light brown humic clayey silts), could be discerned, presumably representing both individual turves and loose soil.

The amount of tumbled masonry encountered suggests that the stonework fronting the rampart must have been fairly substantial, although its foundations were remarkably slight, a trench (117) only 0.10m wide and 0.20m deep, with vertical sides and a flat bottom, filled with tightly packed, large, rounded, waterworn cobbles (076). As these appear to have been adequate support for the revetment masonry (075), it may well have been only an outer skin, a single block thick, presumably integral with the main earthen rampart.

Little of the stonework remained undisturbed, which is perhaps not surprising as the topsoil above it was only 0.18m deep, and the rampart had undoubtedly been extensively robbed (Plate 10). Only the lowest course of stone survived, and that incomplete (Trench C); in some places (Trench G) no masonry at all remained *in situ*. There was, however, a large quantity of tumble spread across the narrow berm between rampart and ditch and also within the final fills of the last re-cut of ditch 220 (214, Phase 3.3). It was possible to distinguish at least five courses of the rampart's stone face (077) which had collapsed outwards, and the amount of tumbled stone in the ditch clearly implies that the revetment wall would originally have been much higher. It was built from dressed but irregular sandstone blocks, with a fair face to the south, keyed presumably into the rampart behind. There was no evidence for mortar, or any other bonding agent, although small patches of clay noted between the stones may have been a last remnant.

The western edge of the turf core of the rampart thinned rapidly, having been severely disturbed in the recent past. Beneath it four fairly distinct deposits were recorded, light grey clay (320) *c* 0.30m thick, patchy greyish black organic silt (318) only 0.05m thick, a small patch of orange grey clay (319) 0.10m thick, and 0.20m of pinkish grey gritty sand (317), presumably representing make-up or foundation levels.

28

The outer face of the rampart extended to within 0.50m of the inner (northern) edge of ditch 220, leaving only a narrow berm between the two. This was effectively flat (Trench C) although in one place (Trench G) it formed a slight hollow (299) filled with organic silty sand (300).

Internal features
Contexts 167, 168, 169, 170, 171, 172, 277/294, 295
There was little opportunity to examine features within the line of the ramparts. Linear feature 172, running north-west to south-east, was part-excavated (Trench C). Although likely to have been truncated by later activity, it was still 2.20m wide at the surface and 0.60m deep. It had a flat bottom 0.50m wide, and the south-western side sloped gently away from the rampart. It seems likely that this feature was a drainage or drip channel to the immediate the rear of the rampart, although this would be difficult to prove. The fills offered little clue to any interpretation; the earliest, 171, comprised homogenous, slightly organic silty clay which was covered by a series of similar orangish brown silty gravels (170, 169, 168, and 167).

On the eastern side of the fort (Trench G) there was a spread of cobbles (277) just to the rear of the rampart, within which a distinct band 1.20m wide (294) ran roughly north-south (approximately parallel to the eastern defensive ditch). The band might represent the last vestige of cobble foundations, either for an internal revetment to the rampart, or for the base of a wall (Plate 11). As most of 277, which may be interpreted as tumble, lay to the west of the wall core, and only the eastern side of band 294 was faced, the former might be a more likely explanation (Plate 12).

Both the layer of cobble tumble and the possible foundations were between 0.20m and 0.30m thick, with individual stones around 0.30m in diameter. They were scattered over a slightly convex metalled surface (295), of which only a strip approximately 2.50m wide survived. Although this feature was almost without doubt of Roman origin, the amount of post-medieval pottery and clay pipe from the general area suggests it had been subject to a considerable amount of modern disturbance, presumably because it was so close to the surface.

The annexe
Context 359, 360, 361, 362
A second ditch, 359, running approximately east-west (Trench N), was excavated some 16m to the east of the fort defences (Trench G: 220). Whilst not physically linked, investigation established the same sequence of re-cuts as for fort ditch 220, strongly suggesting that the ditches were connected in some way, and related to the same periods of activity. Ditch 359 had a V-shaped profile and, like 220, was reduced in width by later re-cuts. It was 1.50m wide at the top and approximately 1.50m deep. Three fills were recorded: black organic material 362, below dark grey, charcoal-flecked homogeneous clay 361, and, in striking contrast to the upper fill of the western ditch, a layer of redeposited natural orange clay (360). The primary fill (362) produced a small assemblage of plant macrofossils (sample 1317) which included a suite of taxa highly suggestive of the presence of short acid grassland, perhaps present as turves. Particularly notable were ?tormentil (*Potentilla cf erecta*) achenes, present in large numbers, together with moderate numbers of heath-grass caryopses, grass culm fragments and some ?grass culm base/rhizome fragments. Invertebrate remains were rare but the records of an elaterid larva (wireworm) abdominal apex, some earthworm egg capsules, and the varied preservation of the insect remains, all fit comfortably with the plant assemblage. Despite the fact that this was a primary ditch fill there was no biological evidence for the presence of water, and the structure of the deposit (so far as it could be determined from one sample) indicated dumped material rather than gradually accumulated sediment.

Although it follows a sequence of changes very similar to that associated with the main fort defences, this ditch seems unlikely to relate to the fort proper, as the southern side and eastern corner of the primary defences clearly lay to the west. It therefore seems possible that ditch 359 and its successors defined the perimeter of a small defended external annexe.

Phase 3.2: Refurbishment of the Fort

The first re-cut of the defensive ditch and outworks
*Contexts 215, 216, 217, **218**/323/411/487/545, 327, 328, 329, 330, 344, 412, 413, 488, **534**, 535, 536, 537*
The first defences (ditch 220, outwork 538) appear to have partly silted, and in part to have been deliberately filled with turves and other dumped rubbish. Ditch 220 was subsequently re-cut (ditch 218), a little inside the original line of the enceinte, the inner edge of the renewed ditch running parallel to, and partly overlapping, that of the earlier defences (220). A yet later re-cut, 214 (Phase 3.3), in turn overlapped 218, making it impossible to establish its full width with any certainty, although it was estimated at about 2.40m. The ditch profile varied from typically V-shaped, sometimes with an eroded 'ankle breaker' (suggested by a break of slope at a depth of about 1.40m (Trenches G and P)), to U-shaped (Trenches C and Q, where it was asymmetrical with a steep inner edge), although the depth remained constant at around 1.70m, unless it had been reduced by modern disturbance (Trench P where it was only 0.95m deep). As with its predecessor, there was a gap in the line of ditch 218 about half way along the southern side.

In general the fills (Fig 7) were very similar in colour, texture and consistency to those of the preceding ditch and must, to a degree, have derived from them. In both of the more deeply excavated sections the primary fills were waterlogged (Trench G: dark grey brown silty clay 217; Trench C: dark greyish brown organic material 330). Elsewhere (Trenches P and Q) they were dry and appeared to diminish in organic content to the west, probably reflecting better drainage and more disturbance (Trench P, 412, dark grey brown silty clay with occasional charcoal flecks; Trench Q, 488, grey brown friable silty clay).

Again the nature of subsequent fills varied along the length of the ditch; within the eastern arm, the primary fill was covered by 216, a very dark grey, plastic, silty clay which incorporated significant amounts of well-preserved wood including artefacts, woodworking debris and roundwood (*see* Chapter 7: Wood, 56), and 215, friable silty clay. On the southern side it was covered by 329, a light grey deposit, and 328, a more mixed clay, and further west (Trench P), by 413, friable, dark brown loamy clay with a few stones.

On the southern side (Trench C) there was, however, a striking change midway through the succession of fills. Fill 328 was covered with a layer of re-deposited natural clay (327) and a 0.10m thick layer of cobbles (344). Both of these not only filled the ditch, but also appear to have been deliberately laid over the berm and up to the face of the rampart (075). It is possible that the defensive ditch had been re-cut rather too close to the ramparts, ultimately causing subsidence. Thus, the layers of clay and cobbles may have served both to level the ditch, and to consolidate the area before the ditch was re-cut for the final time (Phase 3.3, 214).

Palaeoenvironmental evidence from the highly organic primary fill (Trench C: 330, sub-samples 124903 and 124904) shows that heathland and grassland species were the most prominent group, perhaps consistent with the presence of turf either within the deposits or on the surrounding land. The presence of *Juncus squarrosus* seeds in large numbers is of some interest, as this widespread plant is confined to acid soils, particularly wet heaths and bogs, which are perhaps unlikely to have occurred in the Kirkham area in the past and, indeed, are not even recorded in the Fylde in modern times (Perring and Walters 1962). The presence of at least three fig seeds indicates that, to a limited extent, food waste was also probably finding its way into the deposits. On the whole, the insects recovered appeared to originate from natural or semi-natural habitats. The presence of several fragments of stag beetle was of note. This now has a southerly distribution in the British Isles, with some records from central England, but it is absent from northern England, apart from some very isolated records from Cumbria (Clark 1967; Hall 1970) which perhaps require verification, particularly in view of Jessop's (1986, 14) summary of the distribution of the species. There is, however, some evidence for appreciably higher temperatures during the Roman period than those of the present day, which this record would confirm, although the possibility of transportation of insects in hay (for example), within the highly-organised Roman military economy, has to be recognised. Other insect remains included three pronota of a *Tachys* sp, three species of *Aphodius* dung beetles, a single individual of *Oryzaephilus surinamensis* and a specimen of *Hoplia philanthus* (*see* Chapter 7: Plant and Invertebrate Remains, 59).

Fill 216 yielded a somewhat contrasting range of evidence requiring rather different interpretations. Three kinds of water flea resting-eggs, two of them very abundant, and a single ostracod (from sub-sample 110201) testify to aquatic deposition. Evidence from the beetles (single individuals of seven aquatic taxa), and a duckweed seed, offers support for such an interpretation, as does the 'cheesy' texture of the deposit, a description consistent with richly organic and highly humified detrital sediment which formed gradually in a body of still water. The beetles appear to have accumulated from a variety of sources and may largely represent background fauna.

The presence of *Aphodius ?prodromus*, and perhaps also *Oxytelus sculptus*, might indicate dung. This may well have been on adjacent ground surfaces, although the presence of moderate amounts of grass/cereal straw fragments perhaps suggests that at least some stable manure or dung actually found its way into the ditch (there was, however, no evidence of a breeding decomposer community for stable manure and, indeed, decomposers in general were rare). Some of the other beetle species probably also originated in dung, along with others from grain, and a substantial proportion from short vegetation.

The most prominent vegetation types indicated by the plant remains were weed communities and grassland, but there was also a distinctive wetland group, perhaps from marsh or waterside environments (possibly within the ditch itself). There was also a small group of remains from woody plants, alder, birch, oak, hazel and holly, which could represent either nearby woodland or scrub, or imported brushwood. Some probable heathland/moorland plant taxa were also recorded in very small amounts.

In contrast, a second sub-sample (110202) from the same fill (216) produced no evidence for aquatic deposition. As in the first sample, the dung beetle *Aphodius prodromus* was the most numerous beetle, but there was almost no other evidence for foul matter and again decomposers were rare. The remaining beetles seem to have had various origins, either in background fauna or in a very restricted semi-natural habitat. The most abundant plant macrofossils were probably components of turf (?tormentil and heath grass, with many other grass caryopses, and some mosses likely also to have grown in short acid grassland habitats); other plant remains included a few weeds, bracken, and wheat/rye bran, perhaps from stable manure.

Fill 216 could be split into two distinctive components: organic material (sub-sample 131611) and clay (sub-sample 131612). Although the assemblage was rather small, the presence of turves was suggested by some of the plant remains, in particular the abundant pearlwort seeds and the ?grass culm-base/rhizome fragments. The invertebrate assemblage was also limited, but led to a similar conclusion. There were numerous cysts and beetle larvae, and small numbers of water flea resting-eggs, fly puparia and adult flies. The adult beetles, of which there were only 25 individuals, were predominantly taxa from natural or semi-natural habitats, although there was a single *Cryptolestes* sp, probably from grain, along with a consistent trace of wheat/rye bran. In general, the low concentration of remains, high diversity, and large proportion of outdoor forms, suggest an essentially 'background' origin for the beetles and bugs. Although interpretation of this material must remain rather tentative, it may be that turf, or surface soil derived from it, was thrown into the re-cut ditch, gradually becoming mixed with the aquatic sediments.

Despite some underlying similarities between the two assemblages described above, the organic remains from the latter have rather different implications, albeit somewhat tentatively drawn. Both the plants and insects included components which, were they present in larger numbers, might be taken as indicative of the presence of stable manure. Amongst these were wheat/rye bran and whole caryopses, ?wheat chaff, legume flowers, and the beetles *Oxytelus sculptus*, *Monotoma picipes* and *Anthicus floralis* or *formicarius*. It is, however, not impossible that all these remains entered the deposit separately or indirectly, and the main statistics of the insect assemblage, including the decomposers, indicate mixed origins. It could be suggested that the ditch might have acted as a 'dead space' within which wind-blown detritus from surface-deposited dung or manure settled, together no doubt with flying insects. Another group of plants perhaps points to the presence of turves within the deposits, or short grassland close to the ditch, some of the insects perhaps having the same origin.

Like the main ditch system, the possible outwork (538, Phase 3.1) was also probably re-cut during this phase of activity. Ditch 534, 2.20m wide and 0.85m deep, also overlay the inner edge of its predecessor. It contained three fills, the earliest of which, 537, comprised light grey sandy clay containing patches of natural sand, presumably eroded from the ditch sides. This was covered by similar, but slightly more clayey material (536), and a more mixed, possibly disturbed, layer (535), with a gravelly clay lens at its base.

First re-cut of the annexe ditch
Context 352, 353
The first re-cut (352) of annexe ditch 359 also followed roughly the same alignment as its predecessor, although its western end appeared to curve more to the north, perhaps suggesting a terminus and, by extension, an entrance to the annexe. The size and profile of this ditch were very similar to that of ditch 218, its presumed contemporary to the west, around 2.00m wide and 1.40m deep, although, as it curved to the north, it became gradually shallower and narrower, eventually only 1.20m wide and 0.40m deep. In contrast to ditch 218, however, the fill of the re-cut annexe ditch comprised a single deposit of friable, very dark greyish black organic material, 353, perhaps implying rapid backfilling with organic matter.

Phase 3.3: The Second Refurbishment

The second re-cut of the defensive ditch and outworks
Contexts 214/324/421/547, 530, 210, 211, 212, 213, 325, 326, 343, 444, 447, 448, 486, 531, 532, 533/485
The third version of the fort ditch, and refurbishment of the outer works, marks the final stage in the development of the fortifications. As with Phase 3.2, activity was characterised by the excavation of a substantial ditch, the eastern end of which again followed the approximate line of, and cut, the earlier features (220 and 218). The western end, however, ran inside the earlier ditches (seen in

Trench Q), having gradually shifted to the north. No reason for this change in alignment was apparent and, like the earlier ditches, 214 turns north at its western end (Trench Q), maintaining the original line of the defences.

Ditch 214 was generally the same width as its predecessors, c 2.80m (Trenches C and G), although it was up to 1m wider at the western end (Trench Q). Its depth also varied by over 0.50m, from 0.95m to 1.48m. Its profile, however, remained fairly constant, an asymmetrical V-shape, with a break of slope forming a deep and narrow 'ankle breaker' (Plate 14).

The fills of 214 were fairly diverse, although roughly the same sequence of deposition appeared in all of the excavated sections. Three and four fills were noted (Trenches C and G respectively). The earliest (343, 213) was a thick (0.90m) layer of dark grey silty clay. This was covered by a layer which appeared to be a roughly equal mixture of grey brown sandy or silty clay (325, 212) and large, roughly dressed sandstone blocks, undoubtedly fallen masonry from the revetted rampart (075; Plate 15), and thus in reality probably belonging to Phase 4. The sandstone tumble was covered by light grey silt (326, 211), presumably deposited after the collapse of the revetment wall. In places a fourth deposit, 210 (Trench G), lay over the silt. This was an orange-brown silty clay containing fairly frequent rounded cobbles, probably derived from the degradation of 344, the latest fill of the first re-cut (Phase 3.2). To the west (Trench Q) the earliest deposits in the ditch comprised grey clay, 447, apparently localised along the western edge of the cut, and very dark grey organic silt clay, 448, containing a small amount of granular peaty soil and traces of fine charcoal and mortar. The upper fill, 444, obviously the same as 212 and 325 (further east), was 1.12m of mid-grey sandy clay, again mixed with a large number of sandstone blocks.

The final fill of this ditch represents the effective end of Roman activity on the site. The fact that the upper layers contained large amounts of tumble from the collapsed rampart revetment strongly suggests the fort was derelict, or at least in poor repair, by the time the last fills were accumulating.

The outwork ditch was also re-cut again (530, Trench S). Ditch 530 lay within the line of the earlier ditches but was of similar dimensions, c 2.40m wide and 0.70m deep. It contained three fills: dark grey silty clay 531, covered by a thin layer of black, friable silt (532) incorporating a discrete deposit of cobbles (486), and plastic, greyish brown silty clay 533, which appeared either to have collapsed in, or to have been thrown in, from the southern edge of the ditch.

The second re-cut of the annexe ditch
Context 354, 355, 356, 357, 358, 371, 384, 385
As might be expected, the final cut, 354, of the annexe ditch followed approximately the same alignment as its predecessors (359, 352). It contained four fills, the lowest of which comprised a black organic deposit, 358, with no obvious inclusions. This was covered by a thin lens of what appeared to be redeposited natural clay, 357. The two upper layers were both silty clay: 356 was light grey and contained occasional rounded stones and charcoal flecks, and the latest fill, 355, was a darker grey, contained patches of decaying red sandstone, possibly the equivalent of deposits 212, 325, and 444 in ditch 214. An additional stretch of ditch (371; c 3.50m wide and 1.10m deep) to the south-west of ditch 354 (Trench N) contained two fills, a mixed greyish black silt containing patches of redeposited natural (385) below dark grey silty clay 384, and this appeared to be contemporary with 354.

33

Finds

Samian

Only two sherds of samian were recovered from Phase 3.1 contexts. The first, a Dr18/31 from Lezoux, can be dated to the Hadrianic/early Antonine period, but the second is small, and can be dated only to the first century AD. A little over 18% of the total assemblage (30 sherds) derived from layers associated with Phase 3.3, all from the uppermost fills of ditches. The mean sherd size is large, at just under 27g and even if one particularly big sherd (533/1369) weighing 239g is ignored, the average is still over 19g. Both the vessel stamped by Paterclus (Stamp 1) and dated AD 100-120, and the Attianus bowl (Fig 9.10), dated AD 125-145, are almost half vessels and are in relatively good condition, suggesting that they had not been discarded long before deposition. There is, however, still a wide date range, suggesting that much of the samian may be residual.

Coarsewares

Phase 3.1 contexts produced 8% of the stratified pottery from the site, 19 sherds of coarse/fine wares, 15 of amphorae and 24 of mortaria. Only the fill (300) of internal feature 299 produced Black Burnished Ware 1 (Fabric 1), a single fragment of cooking pot, whilst an early fill of ditch 220 (219) produced fragments of an oxidised flagon (Fabric 10). The amphora sherds were all of South Spanish origin (Fabric 20), and the mortaria included a stamped vessel of first century date from the Verulamium region (*see* Chapter 7: Stamp Report, 48), probably residual in this phase. Other sources of supply included South Carlton, Lincoln (Fabric 38, Fig 10.19) again a first century source, and second century Wilderspool material (Fig 10.18).

Phase 3.3 produced 132 sherds, 18% of the stratified pottery from the site. The majority came from annexe ditches 354 (54 sherds) and 371 (59 sherds). Only three sherds of Black Burnished Ware 1 (Fabric 1) were noted, whilst greywares (Fabric 11) included a variety of jars (Figs 10.21–25), all consistent with a late first or second century date, and a lid (Fig 10.26) of similar date; a fill (533) of the final outwork ditch produced a rough-cast beaker (Fig 10.20) dated *c* AD 80-130/5. Amphora fragments included South Spanish Fabric 20 and a Gaulish vessel (Fig 10.27). Mortaria sherds were products of Wilderspool and the Verulamium region.

Post-Roman pottery

Two fragments of ostensibly medieval pottery were recovered from the footings and tumble of the cobble foundation for wall 294 (276, 277, Phase 3.1); the presence of medieval material here might imply stone robbing. A further fragment of a post-medieval vessel was recovered from a Phase 3.1 ditch fill (219); since, however, it appears to derive from a primary fill, it is likely that it was intrusive.

Other finds

A small, irregularly made melon bead of turquoise frit was recovered from cobble tumble 277 (Phase 3.1). Such beads are normally associated with the first and second centuries AD, although they have a very long life, reappearing in the early medieval period when small, ill-made beads such as this one predominate. It would, however, seem reasonable to assign this particular example to the Roman period, although the possibility of later robbing, raised with regard to the presence of medieval pottery fragments within the same context, should be noted. A fragment of a typical square glass storage bottle from ditch 371 can be dated to the first or second century.

Metalwork from this phase comprised only a copper alloy brooch fragment (probably a Colchester derivative) of first or early second century date, from wall footings 276 (Phase 3.1), and four fragments of iron: a small fragment of nail from fill 300 (linear feature 299), another nail and a large U-shaped object, possibly a shackle of the kind associated with carts (Manning 1986, eg S104, S105) both from 355, a Phase 3.3 ditch fill, and a small fragment of strip from its contemporary outwork (fill 533).

Six fragments of incidentally fired clay, probably deriving from hearths or kiln superstructure, were recovered from linear feature 171 and cobble tumble 277 (both Phase 3.1). Two other small fragments of vitrified hearth lining were also found (one from fill 533 the other from ditch 371, Phase 3.3). Ditch 371 also contained a small amount of burnt clay, again possibly associated with industrial processes.

A small amount of tile and brick was also recovered, most from Phase 3.3. It indicates that debris from substantial buildings was incorporated in the fills of the latest re-cut of the fort ditch, reinforcing the impression that material accumulated as, or after, the fort fell into decline.

Wood

Most of the worked wood derived from Phase 3.2, almost entirely from a single fill (216) of the first recut of the ditch (218). There was, however, also a small amount from ditch 220 (fills 332, 219, Phase 3.1), accumulated early in the life of the stone fort. The five fragments from 332, although badly preserved, appear to represent primary conversion waste, clearly implying the on-site preparation of timber, although the amount present is very small. The single fragment from 219 is likely to be discarded demolition debris.

The remainder of the wood forms a distinct group, probably deposited as one, within a confined area in ditch 218. It represents a large number of tent pegs, probably in excess of 40, although many are now fragmentary or incomplete. A single, excellently preserved *pilum muralis* (Fig 11; Plate 16) was deposited with the group, as were a few small pegs. Little or no waste wood or woodworking debris was recovered with this group, suggesting that it is a dump of completed, surplus or unfit objects rather than clearance from their production. Many of the pegs appear to have been used, presumably in the earlier phases, possibly in one of the temporary camps.

Discussion

Phase 3 encompasses the construction and lifetime of the stone fort, probably built around the end of the first, or early second, century AD, perhaps as an adjunct to troop movements following the evacuation of Scotland in *c* AD 87 (D Shotter, pers comm) Again, the large element of residual material within the assemblage precludes precise dating.

The southern side of the defences was examined in some detail. It comprised a stone-revetted clay and turf rampart some 4.5m wide, fronted by a single ditch which was re-cut twice, on slightly differing alignments, during the lifetime of the fort. There were apparent outworks to the west of the main fort, which echoed the outline of the defences some 10m or more further out. It seems likely that these defences are part of the same circuit encountered in earlier excavations, when Pickering reported a ditch some 30 feet (9.1m) wide (Singleton 1980). At the time of its discovery this ditch was not fully excavated, and it is likely that the three successive ditch lines were conflated into a single feature by the excavator. Pickering also recorded a ditch with cobbled berm (*op cit*) running north-south, which presumably represented the western side of the fort in Phase 3.2, as a layer of cobbles was noted over the berm during this period. The dressed red sandstone outer face of the rampart had clearly been heavily robbed (Plate 13), and survived only as a single incomplete course of masonry on clay and cobble foundations, with a large amount of tumbled and smashed stone within the latest fills of the last ditch (Plate 15).

A similar stretch of three successive ditches was found east of the fort proper. In the main, the ditches lay either outside the excavation boundary or in areas of modern disturbance, and in consequence the area bounded by them was not examined. The most obvious explanation for their existence, however, would be as part of a fortified annexe. External annexes appear to be relatively common in the North West, and have been reported from a number of sites, including Ribchester, up-river to the east (Olivier 1987, Buxton and Howard-Davis forthcoming).

There is little evidence of structures within the principal defensive enceinte, although part of the cobbled surfaces might represent a heavily-robbed internal revetment to the rampart. There is, in fact, ample evidence for extensive and prolonged disturbance in this area, and it seems reasonable to suggest that a substantial source of dressed stone in an area of boulder clay would not have been long overlooked. Whilst it cannot be proved, the incorporation of a Roman tombstone within the fabric of the medieval church at Kirkham (probably Norman in origin, but re-built in 1512 and then almost entirely replaced between 1822 and 1853) might suggest that much of its fabric derived ultimately from the fort defences (Croston 1893, 360). It is, indeed, tempting to see the albeit unstratified fragments of potentially thirteenth-century pottery recovered from cleaning layer 287 as evidence for this.

It seems clear that the stone-built fort replaced, or incorporated, the signal station/fortlet (Phase 2) that previously stood on the site. The ditches of this appreciably smaller structure appear to have been filled at or by this point, and some of the internal structure demolished, as several substantial postholes lay beneath the turf and clay rampart. Recent excavations at Burgh-by-Sands (Daniels 1989) revealed a small round signal tower subsumed into in a more conventional rectangular turf and timber fort (Burgh 1). In that case it could be demonstrated that the tower continued in use, possibly as part of a modified entrance, and it is indeed likely that the western line of the Phase 2 enclosure at Kirkham was fossilised as part of a southern entrance to the fort, perhaps adding to the argument for its continued use in Phase 3.

Such continuity might suggest that there had never been a full-size turf and timber fort on the hilltop at Kirkham and certainly no evidence for such is as yet forthcoming. Thus it can be postulated that the increase in the size of the military establishment at this time must have reflected a major change in purpose, status, or garrison, associated with the period of refurbishment and retrenchment which is generally accepted to have occurred in the last years of the first century AD or the early years of the second. It has been suggested (Casey 1992) that this extensive programme of re-building in part symbolised the Roman acceptance of a permanent presence in Britain. Such activity must, surely, have signalled a new continuity of contact and, by extension, have established an enhanced potential for longer-term commercial relationships between the army and the local populace. In terms of Kirkham, this could suggest a change of role from coastal watch and supply depot/entrepot to redistributive centre, servicing somewhat more than the immediate need of garrisons in the area, thereby seeking to establish Kirkham as a market centre. It is of interest that this happened at a time when, in Ribchester, buildings along the line of the road from Kirkham appear to have been connected in some way with trade or the movement of merchandise, and even perhaps of military control over it (Buxton and Howard-Davis forthcoming). Such a role must have necessitated an increased movement of trade goods presumably by sea, since the fort appears to have looked coastwards.

The fort at Kirkham appears to have been abandoned around the middle of the second century AD, coinciding closely with a severe decline in activity at Ribchester and reinforcing the close link between the two forts. It is assumed that the later fills of the last re-cut ditch reflect the subsequent abandonment and decay, and thus presumably accumulated over a considerable period. Thornber, writing in the early-nineteenth century (Singleton 1980, 1) implies that some, at least, of the fort was still visible above ground at that time. The fort stood within the town fields and would presumably have been extensively robbed over the centuries, although not apparently completely cleared until a comparatively late date.

CHAPTER 6
THE EXTRAMURAL AND LATER ACTIVITY

Phase 2/3

Excavation in the lower-lying southern part of the site was made extremely difficult by extensive waterlogging and a number of modern factors, including spilled heating fuel. It proved impossible to make any direct stratigraphic links between archaeological remains there (Trenches D, H, E, L and M) and any of the other significant features on the site, effectively separating the remains of the signal station/fortlet and the later fort from most of the features which appeared to represent extramural activity. Thus, the association of features in this area with those of either phase of the apparently permanent military complex (Phases 2 and 3) relies heavily on their orientation and alignment, and on dating evidence. Most have been assigned only generally to Phase 2/3 and inevitably there were also several isolated features which proved impossible to assign to a particular phase. Phase 3 appears to represent the longest period of activity, and it is thus likely that the majority of the features excavated in the southern part of the site pertain to that phase. Few, if any, of the events represented, however, would have coincided precisely with the sequence of building and rebuilding charted in the fort.

Possible industrial activity
*Contexts **406**, 407, **414**, 415, 416, **417**, 418, 419, 420, 428, **429**, 430, 431, **433**, 440, 441, **442**, 443, 449, 450*
A large hollow (429) cutting the natural clays towards the centre of the site (Trench M) was irregular in plan but at least 5m in diameter and *c* 0.40m deep, with steeply sloping sides and a relatively flat base (Fig 8). At its eastern edge a narrow (*c* 1m wide), gently sloping ramp appeared to give access to the centre. The primary fill (431), a patchy deposit of friable, black, silty clay up to 0.16m thick, gave the impression of being some kind of industrial residue and sample 1253 produced a trace of charcoal and some small fragments of slag. To the east, fill 431 was cut by a somewhat amorphous feature (442), tentatively identified as the remnants of a badly damaged hearth. About 1m across and 0.22m deep, this was filled by dark grey silty clay (440) and a thin lens of lighter grey, sandier material (441). Elsewhere, fill 431 was covered by mottled, apparently oxidised, orange clay (430), perhaps with some ash. Much of 430 was covered in turn by two substantial and similar deposits of riverworn cobbles (418, 420) in a very dark grey, silty clay matrix.

The steep sides of hollow 429 might imply that it did not form naturally, and the apparent ramp could be seen as the deliberate creation of an easy access point. The nature of the primary fill strongly suggests an association with some kind of high temperature process, whilst the latest fill, clay and cobbles, may represent an attempt to level the area at a later date, after it had gone out of use. The final fill of 429 (420) was cut by, or contemporary with, ditch 433 (the relationship was not clear), running north-south, which lay to the immediate west of the hollow. This feature, some 2.50m wide and *c* 1m deep, with steeply sloping sides and a gently concave base, contained two fills: 450, very wet, grey clay containing a large amount of organic material and some building debris, below 449, a greyish brown silty clay very similar to 418, the cobble fill of 429. The small segment excavated proved difficult to set within a context.
Palaeoenvironmental analysis of fill 450 (sample 1256) suggested that it might have been deposited in water, but there were too few other invertebrates to define the conditions within the ditch any more closely. No truly aquatic plant taxa were recorded, although several species from wet meadows or ditch banks were present. The most abundant were stinging nettles, perhaps indicative of seasonally wet ground with a high nutrient status or nearby rubbish deposits,

but there were also some possible grassland plants and other taxa of disturbed habitats. The small group of insects might have originated from grazing land or dung from animals fed with cereals. A single fig seed hints at the presence of human faecal material.

Wall 417, which lay between hollow 429 and ditch 433, was represented by the last remnant of foundations, less than 0.20m deep. It, too, ran north-south; the northern extent was destroyed by modern foundations and the southern end faded out towards the centre of the area. The foundations, about 1m wide, comprised rounded, riverworn cobbles (0.25m in diameter) set in a shallow bedding trench (554) containing mid-brown sandy clay 419. Tumble (428) spread outwards on both sides of the wall and, like the wall proper, it faded out towards the south. The stone used for these footings was similar to that in the foundations of the sandstone rampart revetment (Phase 3) and thus it is possible that they, too, supported a masonry wall. All other evidence for the nature of the structure had been destroyed by later activity. No obvious floor surface survived, although the wall was most likely to have been associated with a building, and probably also with ditch 433 to the west. The erection of this building may have, in fact, provided the impetus to level up the fills of 429, providing a relatively level work surface. An area of compacted, very dark greyish brown material containing slag and angular stones (443), immediately to the west of wall 417, suggests industrial activity in the close vicinity.

Two other linear features, both cut into natural clays, lay in the same area (Trench M), although they did not appear to be related to any of the other features. The first, 406, was a shallow east-west slot (0.40m wide, 0.06m deep) filled with dark brown silty clay (407). The second, 414, was also aligned east-west (up to 2.23m wide, 0.30m deep) with a shallow V-shaped profile. It contained two fills, 416, 0.09m of dark grey silty clay, and 415, a similar silty clay but with numerous rounded stones and gravel.

The possible road
Contexts 133, 134, 138, **139/158**, 204, 207, **268**, 269, 270, 271, **303/334**, **335**, **340/341**, **345**, 346, **366**
Layer 366 (Trench L) was the largest and probably the best preserved area of metalling, made from small rounded river pebbles (90%) set in a plastic grey clay matrix. It reached a maximum thickness of 0.20m at its southern edge, where the pebbles lay directly upon natural clay. It was associated with 345, a ditch 1.30m wide and 0.20m deep, lying about 1m to the south, presumably a drainage gully. This was filled by 346, dark grey brown, sandy clay containing a few charcoal flecks and c 20% small rounded pebbles, which had probably eroded from the road surface.

A very similar, possibly identical surface (335) was seen to the east (Trenches E and H). Initially it appeared to respect the southern edge of ditch 006 (Phase 1.3), but excavation established that the thin but compact band of pebbles actually spread over the latest fill of the ditch. In the same area (over 006), 335 was covered by a layer of brownish grey silty clay (303), which had presumably accumulated over the road surface during its use.

Other patches of metalling were less well preserved. In the south-eastern part of the area (Trench H) a patch of pebbles in a grey brown silty clay matrix (340) lay directly above the natural subsoil and gradually thinned towards the east (Trench D). In the same area a layer of mottled, dark yellowish brown material (139), containing a large amount of stones (c 0.05m diameter) (158), lay over the upper fills of hollow 135 (Phase 1.1). It also appeared to fill 138, a small, shallow linear feature (0.55m wide, by 0.05m deep) with gently sloping sides and a flat base, which ran south at right angles to the corner of 135. To the south, a similar patch of pebbles, 204 (roughly 4.30m by 2.00m), overlay natural subsoils. It gradually faded westwards, becoming a layer of dark brown sandy silt (268) similar to 139. Removal of 268 exposed what appeared to be a small, badly truncated, oval posthole (269), 0.63m in diameter. Although only the bottom 0.07m of this feature survived, it contained two fills, grey brown silty clay 270, below sandy silt 271. Another spread of metalling, 207, lay somewhat to the north.

If the scattered patches of metalling in this area (Trenches D and E/H) were originally continuous, then the appearance of surface 268 would suggest that it was contemporary with surfaces 335 and 366. It was covered by 0.18m of greyish orange clay (134), which was covered in turn by what appeared to be a dump of largish cobbles, up to c 0.35m in diameter (133). The stratigraphic relationship between this and the Phase 1 ditches appeared to reinforce the suggestion that ditches 052, 006 and 056 had all fallen into disuse and become filled before being sealed beneath a metalled road surface, probably associated with the Phase 3 fort. The deposition of clay and large cobbles might imply deliberate levelling after the surface had subsided as it ran over the softer ditch fills.

Extramural domestic activity
Contexts **008**, 009, **018**, 019, **020**, 021, **025**, 026, **030**, 031, 040, 041, **044**, 045, **046**, 047, **048**, 049, **050**, 051, **054**, 055, 072, 073, 074, **085**, **086**, 087, **094**, 095, **096**, 097, **106**, 107, **130**, 131, **187**, 188
In the easternmost part of the site (Trench A) three broadly similar groups of features could be identified. The first lay directly below topsoil, and cut the upcast (012) from ditch 052 (Phase 1.2). All, therefore, clearly post-dated Phase 1, although they had no other recognisable stratigraphic relationships. Most of the features within this group were somewhat amorphous and may have been formed naturally. There was no obvious discernible pattern in the group, and no clear stratigraphic links could be made between them. They comprised: 048, a lozenge-shaped feature (0.30m wide and 0.30m deep), filled by 049, grey brown silty clay; 050, a shallow, circular feature (0.12m in diameter and 0.02m deep), filled by silty clay 051, similar to 049; 054 (fill 055); 085, a small patch of sub-rounded stones; and, finally, 130, an irregular, sub-circular feature (c 0.89m in diameter and 0.11m deep), filled with sandy clay (131). Three linear features also fell into this group: 018, c 0.41m wide and 0.04m deep and filled with greyish brown silty clay (019); 020, aligned east-west (0.51m wide and 21m deep) filled by 021, mid-grey silty clay; and 187, a shallow but steep-sided feature (0.60m wide and 0.10m deep) filled by 188, dark grey loamy clay.

The second group of features (Trench A) was again later than Phase 1, but otherwise could not be dated and again no pattern could be discerned. These features cut either ditch 052, or 023, the foundation trench for its possible palisade (see above, Phase 1.2). Three of the four features in this group had no further stratigraphic relationships, but the fourth was cut by a later hollow (040). Features 008 and 106 both cut the fills of ditch 052. The former was curvilinear (0.33m wide and 0.13m deep) with a U-shaped profile. It was filled by 009, a relatively compact silty clay containing occasional small rounded stones and a few charcoal flecks. The latter (106) was a small tapering posthole (0.20m diameter, 0.15m deep) filled by grey brown silty clay 107. Linear feature 025 lay to the north-west of the above. It clearly cut palisade trench 023, and was 0.78m wide and 0.36m deep. It was filled by mid to light grey clay 026, and a small pile of large stones (c 0.30m by 0.18m). The last feature in this group, 044, was another wide (0.33m), shallow (0.08m) linear cut, filled by 045, a brownish grey silty clay. This feature was itself cut by 040, an amorphous hollow of probably natural origin, although filled by 041, a patch of charcoal.

The third series of features all cut ditch 004 (Trench A, Phase 1.3). The first of them, slot 096, ran north-east to south-west, at an angle to the earlier linear features, which ran north-south or east-west. It was 0.72m wide and 0.23m deep, with gently sloping sides and a dark grey slightly sandy clay fill (097). A second slot, 094, ran roughly east-west; to the west it cut slot 096, whilst to the east it came to a slightly irregular, rounded end. It was 0.61m wide, 0.05m deep, with a flat base, and was filled by coarse, gritty, mottled yellowish-grey clay, 095. Hollow 030, part of which was covered by the baulk, lay over the intersection of ditches 004 and 006 (Phase 1.3). It was around 2.40m in diameter and relatively shallow (0.15m) with two fills; the earliest, 072, a layer of small to medium rounded pebbles, appeared to have sunk, or been compacted, into the underlying ditch fill. The pebbles were covered by 031, greyish brown gritty and clayey sand. The possibility that this feature might represent a sunken-floored post-Roman building cannot be ruled out, but this appears unlikely as it resembles a depression (possibly caused by subsidence at the ditch intersection) rather than a deliberately cut feature.

A small posthole, 086, was cut through the upper fill of hollow 030. It was 0.32m in diameter and 0.46m deep, and filled with greyish brown silty loam (087) containing charcoal flecks. Another two, rather more stratigraphically isolated, features were examined (Trench A). North-south linear feature, 046, filled with silty brown clay, 047, was cut roughly at right angles by 073, a similar feature with a similar clay fill, 074. Although few of these features fall into recognisable groups, their morphology and the finds recovered from their fills suggest that the activity in this area was generally domestic in nature.

Other features
Contexts 279, 280, 296, 297, 496, 497, 516, 519, 521, 522, 523, 524, 525, 526, 548, 551, 552
Several other isolated features, probably of Roman origin, have no obvious interpretation. For most of them stratigraphic relationships were with the natural subsoil and topsoil only and they are therefore simply listed here: a single, flat bottomed pit (Trench F: 280); a small lozenge-shaped pit (296) in the vicinity of metalled surface 335 (Trench H); a linear feature (Trench W: 548); a large, steep-sided pit (Trench R: 496). Clearly of Roman date, it was possibly associated with extramural activity. West of the Phase 2 signal station/fortlet (Trench T), a short stretch of a possibly Roman ditch, 516, lay isolated from ditch 513 (Phase 2.2). Although there is insufficient evidence for certainty, this raises the possibility of a further outwork. There were, however, also several modern features in this part of the site. Three features in the far south-western corner of the site (Trench V: 522, 524; Trench Z: 551) appeared badly truncated.

Finds

Samian
Thirty-three sherds, c 20% of the samian from the site, were recovered from the extramural area. The mean sherd size of 9.6g is smaller than average, and the pottery is very mixed, comparing generally in date range with material from the other phases, including some of the earliest material, as well as Hadrianic/Antonine sherds. Although there was still a considerable amount of residual material within the extramural assemblage, as might be expected, the number of later sherds was slightly greater than in the Phase 1 group.

Coarsewares
In total, 66 sherds of coarse/fine wares, 22 of amphorae, and six of mortaria, around 13% of the stratified pottery were recovered from the extramural area. The vessels represented included a ring-neck flagon (Fabric 12) of late first/early second century date from fill 021, and an everted rim bowl (also Fabric 12) from layer 139. Black Burnished Ware 1 was recovered from fills 055 and 072 and layer 139, suggesting a second century date. All the amphora sherds are of South Spanish Fabric 20. Sources of supply for mortaria include Wilderspool (Fabrics 30, 36), Verulamium (Fabric 32), and the Gallo-Belgic region (Fabric 37). The

Verulamium and Gallo-Belgic regions were significant sources of supply in the late first century.

Post-Roman pottery
Two fragments of post-medieval pottery were recovered from road surface 340, suggesting later disturbance.

Other finds
Only three fragments of glass were recovered from the extramural area. Single fragments from linear features 020 and 045 were undiagnostic but probably Roman, whilst that from 054 (fill 055) is without doubt of nineteenth century date and adds to the evidence for extensive late disturbance.

Only three fragments of wood were recovered, from 450, a fill of ditch 443, and 497, a fill of pit 496. All three fragments appear to be rough, in one case a substantial fragment of trunk. The fragment from 450 was burnt and, since it derived from a layer full of demolition debris and organic waste, may again suggest the use of scrap wood as fuel, or alternatively the disposal of demolition waste.

A single fragment of folded scrap lead sheet came from 431, a hollow connected with some industrial process, and evidence for smithing derived from 026, the fill of a late linear feature, and uncharacterised debris came from layer 139. Small, and probably insignificant amounts of fired clay also came from fills 072 and 346. A total of 76 fragments of mixed tile and brick derived from 21 contexts, for the most part evenly spread with no obvious concentrations. Again, few conclusions can be drawn from this material except to note evidence for tiled roofs (both *imbrex* and *tegula*) and box tile.

Phase 4: Medieval and Later Activity

Possible medieval features
Contexts 445, 446, 453, 454, 455, 460, 461,
The presence, in the finds assemblage, of several relatively unabraded fragments of medieval pottery suggests, not unsurprisingly, a medieval presence in the vicinity, probably associated with stone robbing and agriculture. Four features have been assigned to this period.

A single ditch, 460, was recognised to the west of the Phase 3 outworks (Trench S). Aligned north-south, it was approximately 0.70m wide and 0.28m deep and was filled by 461, dark grey silty sand containing a few small rounded pebbles. No firm date can be assigned, although it was clearly later than the three superimposed outwork ditches (530, 534, 538). It appeared to align closely with a similar feature to the east (Trench Q: 445) and may thus have been contemporary.

Ditch 445 without doubt cut ditch 421 (Phase 3.3), and was, therefore, definitely later in date, probably post-Roman. It was 1.70m wide and 0.35m deep with relatively steep sides and a flat bottom, and was filled by 446, dark grey brown clay loam. Posthole 453, and small linear pebble spread 455 close by, were probably of a similar date. The posthole (0.19m in diameter and 0.12m deep) was filled by a friable, dark brown silty clay (454), containing, especially around the edges, a number of sub-rounded stones, presumably post packing. The stone spread (455), tightly packed small and medium-sized pebbles, ran north-west to south-east. The presence of medieval pottery types within the fills of these features confirms the medieval date, and it is suggested that they may represent land boundaries.

Late features
The numerous late features are described in the archive. For a list, see
Summary Context Index, Appendix 1.

Discussion

Evidence for activity outside the fort is disparate and inconclusive. There is no
doubt, however, that the features beyond its confines represented a significant
level of activity and spanned at least the existence of the signalling station/fortlet
and the stone fort, and may well have continued in existence beyond (Singleton
1980, 8) into the third century.

Little coherent structure could be detected amongst the groups of features,
although one or more metalled surfaces appear to have covered significant
portions of the site and may relate to the road surface observed by Pickering in
1958 (*op cit*, 3).

There appears to be some evidence for industrial activity, in the form of debris-
filled hollow 429 and hearth 442, which might be associated with a building or
enclosure represented in nebulous form by shallow ditches and cobble
foundations. Although no great amount of evidence survives, secondary iron-
working seems the most likely activity.

Other features have been characterised as generally domestic in nature and may
represent the very last remnants of domestic compounds and buildings. Almost
nothing can be adduced of their appearance except for the continued presence of
brick and tile debris in relatively large amounts, and the marked absence of nails,
which might be expected in quantity if there were Roman-style timber-framed
buildings in the vicinity. A single cobble and clay foundation might suggest
wattle and daub or cob construction but, it must be noted, the sandstone rampart
revetment stood on insubstantial cobble and clay footings which, without the
survival of coursed masonry above, would have given little clue to the
substantial nature of the wall.

Whilst most of the generally small quantities of finds from the site come from
Phase 2/3 contexts, no particular activity in this area was undertaken over a
prolonged period. Bearing in mind the amount of disturbance, a greater density
of finds might have been expected, even in the topsoil, had there been prolonged
or continuous activity.

Conventionally this area would have been interpreted as part of the extramural
civilian settlement associated with the site. Recent research, however, is now
leading to the conclusion that, in their early days at least, Roman military
establishments were in fact extremely introverted, importing their traditional
culture wholesale and interacting very rarely with the local populace (Casey
1992, 97). Evidence from Ribchester (Buxton and Howard-Davis forthcoming)
indeed suggests that the civilian population was systematically kept at some
distance from the fort, not only by the maintenance of a clear *cordon sanitaire*
beyond the defences, but also by the instigation of a military-dominated 'contact
zone' with workshops and stabling, between the fort and the civilian settlement.
Sparse as it is, the evidence from Kirkham might fit into the same context, with a
relatively open area dotted with small work compounds, suggesting that any
true civilian settlement must lie elsewhere. Presumably its existence would have
been drastically affected by the sudden abandonment of the fort in the mid-
second century, but since it could have continued to service the wider
population, this impact would have been manifest as a slow wind-down and
contraction, rather than an abrupt end.

There is reason to believe that Kirkham existed in some form by the seventh century AD (Singleton 1980), and it is without doubt pre-Conquest in origin, as it appears as *Chicheham* (settlement by the church) in the Domesday Survey (Hinde 1986). This might suggest a low-level continuity of settlement from the Roman period despite the demise of the fort, especially as the ridge upon which Dowbridge stands is dry in a very wet and low-lying area. Further, as a concentration of population providing a focal point within an area of extremely sparse settlement, it might well have provided an attraction and impetus for the foundation of an early medieval religious establishment.

CHAPTER 7
THE FINDS

Introduction

Since it was clear from the start of the project that the overall density of finds from the site would be thin, a policy of total collection was adopted in an attempt to maximise the level of information retrieval. Most of the excavated area was dry, but some of the deeper ditch sections were heavily waterlogged, leading to excellent preservation of organic objects within their fills. All material has been catalogued but not all catalogues are published here. Those omitted, generally bulk material such as tile and brick, and post-Roman finds, are available in the site archive. Where necessary for the interpretation of the site, however, mention has been made both within the narrative, and below, of all finds groups. Individual finds are identified by context and by object record number (OR), which effectively provides an inventory of all finds, samples etc from the site. They appear in the format context/OR (eg 011/1039) and are followed by an indication of the phase of activity from which the find derives. All catalogues appear in phase (chronological) order. Where tables and catalogues add little to the discussion they appear in Appendix 2. This is noted within the text.

Hand-Made Pottery

Seven vessel fragments in a coarse hand-made fabric were recovered from Phase 1.4 contexts. Although there is little or no Iron Age material for comparison from this area, it can be suggested that the fabric resembles material from late Iron Age/Romano-British sites a little further south (N Neil, pers comm) and can be tentatively assigned a similar date.

The fabric
Hard-fired, hand-made. Brown surfaces and darker core. Very mixed temper, ill sorted up to *c* 2mm. Calcite(?) and mica, voids. Occasional very large grits. Surfaces slightly burnished.

Samian (J Mills)

The samian assemblage was small, only 162 sherds (2.368kg) representing a minimum of 154 vessels. Samian was recovered from Phases 1.1 - 1.5, 3.1, 3.3, and Phase 2/3 (the extramural area), as well as from modern levels. All material was examined, identified, and where possible dated.

The surfaces of much of the pottery were badly eroded by the ?acidic and waterlogged soil conditions. In many cases only one side of the sherd was affected, suggesting that its orientation in the ground was the principal factor influencing surface erosion. The fabrics were also affected by the soil conditions, which have altered their colour. Obviously this has meant that the identification of both decorative detail and production centre (fabric) was unusually difficult. In addition, because of this damage, no valid observation could be made on the degree of use/wear of the pottery.

Fabrics
Material from both Southern (La Graufesenque and Montans) and Central (Les Martres-de-Veyre and Lezoux) Gaul was identified; no Eastern Gaulish wares were noted. The relative proportions from each production centre, based on minimum vessel number, are as follows:

Southern Gaul	La Graufesenque	45.5%
	Montans	0.5%
Central Gaul	Les Martres-de-Veyre	16.0%

Lezoux, pre-export fabric   2.0%
Lezoux, main export period   38.0%

Almost 50% of the samian is from La Graufesenque, analysis of the vessel forms suggesting that it is entirely of Flavian or Flavian/Trajanic date. Pre-export Lezoux and Les Martres-de-Veyre wares produced during the Trajanic period were, for the first decade of the second century, exported to Britain alongside Southern Gaulish wares. Together they bring the quantity of samian in the assemblage which was produced prior to the main export period at Lezoux (ie pre-*c* AD 120) to around 60%. The quantity of Les Martres products recognised here is slightly higher than is usual for British sites, around 10% being more normal. It is of interest that, at Kirkham, Lezoux wares account for less than 40% of the assemblage. In general more Lezoux wares than Southern Gaulish products would be expected from a site occupied during the first and second centuries AD.

Sherds from three vessels were identified in pre-export period Lezoux fabric. All have a pale, highly micaceous fabric, and the remaining slip is thin and of a matte orangey colour. Stray sherds in this fabric are usually accounted for by the suggestion that the vessels were personal possessions, probably of military personnel, and came to the site as such. A group of Trajanic Lezoux ware from excavations at the new cemetery site at Rocester, Staffordshire may, however, indicate that some early Lezoux ware was exported to Britain (B Dickinson, pers comm), and the occurrence of three vessels at Kirkham may be further evidence of this trade.

A single sherd of second century Montans ware was recovered. Increasing, if still small, quantities of this late South Gaulish ware are being recognised from other sites in the North West, including Wilderspool, Chester, Manchester, Carlisle and Ribchester (Dickinson forthcoming), perhaps suggesting direct import to, and distribution from, a western port such as Chester.

Forms
The range of forms present is shown in Table 1; all are Dragendorf (Dr) unless otherwise stated. The quantification represents minimum number of vessels identified.

No pre-Flavian forms were recovered and, of the 60 decorated bowls represented, only three definite, and one possible, Form 29 bowls were identified. This form was out of production by *c* AD 85, and the hemispherical bowl, Form 37, emerged *c* AD 70 to become the most common decorated bowl by the early AD 80s, as can be seen by the relative proportions of the two forms at Pompeii (Atkinson 1914). The style of decoration of the two most closely dateable Form 29 bowls from the site puts them at the very end of production for the form (AD 75-85). Of the 26 Southern Gaulish Form 37 bowls, 12 can be dated more closely than 'Flavian' or 'Flavian/Trajanic'. Two were produced *c* AD 70-85 and another two *c* AD 75-100. The remaining eight date to AD 80-100. This seems to indicate that increasing quantities of material came to the site towards the end of the first century AD.

Cups, dishes, bowls and a few closed forms are present, but none of them are forms which were introduced after about AD 160. The flanged bowl, Form 38, a form most popular in the second half of the second century, is notable for its absence, and straight-sided cup Form 33 is rare at this site. This was the most popular cup in the second century and had completely replaced its predecessor, Form 27, by about AD 160. Only three vessels are represented: two of Hadrianic/Antonine date, and the single Form 33a from Les Martres-de-Veyre is Trajanic.

Form	1:1	1:2	1:3	1:4	1:5	3:1	3:2	3:3	2/3	Unph	Mod	Total
15/17 or 18			1	2				2	1	2		8
15/17R or 18				1								1
18		1		3				2	2	1		9
18R									1			1
18/31	4	1		2		1		5	4	2		19
18/31R	2							2				4
27	1			1				1	1	4		8
29		1	1						1			3
29 or 37				1								1
30				1					1	1		3
30 or 37			1	2				2	2	1		8
33	1			1								2
33a									1			1
36					1							1
37	1	4	2	13				12	7	7		46
Curle 11								1	1	1		3
Bowl									1			1
Dish			1						4			5
Dish or bowl		1							2	2		5
Cup				1								1
Closed form										3		3
Unident.	1	4	1	4	1				3	3	4	21

Table 1: Samian vessel form by Phase

Dating

The stratigraphic distribution of the samian shows no distinct chronological progression. This suggests extensive re-working of the deposits, presumably during the various phases of re-modelling of the complex, resulting in the mixing of earlier and later material.

It can be seen from the range and comparative quantities of the different forms present, as well as from the relative proportions by production centre, that there is no material on the site pre-dating the Flavian period and none later than c AD 160. The first samian coming to the site was produced around AD 70-85. It is noteworthy that, unlike Ribchester (Dickinson forthcoming), no pre-Flavian wares were recognised in this assemblage, and this may indicate that the first Roman presence at Kirkham was established slightly later than at Ribchester. A date in the late AD 70s or early in the next decade is possible.

The samian supply seems to have declined little, if at all, towards the end of the La Graufesenque export period; there was no apparent halt in the supply of samian to the site at the end of the first century. Indeed, the relatively high percentage of vessels from Les Martres-de-Veyre and the presence of Trajanic Lezoux ware indicate that supply continued throughout the Trajanic period. Little (only five vessels) of the samian from the main export period at Lezoux can be dated particularly closely. The vast majority, however, can be assigned to the Hadrianic/Antonine period and it is probable that very little, if any, was produced later than AD 150. Neither the decorated wares of Paternus and Cinnamus, nor the plain forms common in the second half of the second century, are represented in the group. Closely dated pieces from the uppermost fills of the second re-cut (214) of the fort ditch (212, 355, 533, Phase 3.3) include some of the largest sherds from the site, two of which are almost half vessels: Stamp 1 (Fig 9.13) of Trajanic date, and a Form 37 bowl of Attianus (Fig 9.10) dated AD 125-145. Despite the erosion of the external surface of the latter, the interior exhibits no signs of wear, and this may indicate that it was in use for only a short time before deposition. When considered together this evidence suggests that the fort was abandoned during the middle years of the second century.

Use and re-use

Comment on vessel wear is precluded by the poor survival of samian from the site. It is perhaps of interest, however, that there is no evidence from the group for the secondary use of sherds as described by Marsh (1981, 229). Only three sherds had been drilled for riveted repairs, all Form 37 bowls, one Southern Gaulish, one from Les Martres-de-Veyre (Fig 9.7) and the pre-export Lezoux bowl (Fig 9.9). Significantly all of the repaired bowls were produced before *c* AD 120.

Summary
The analysis of the forms and fabrics of the samian indicates that it was produced between *c* AD 70 and AD 150 at the latest. The mixed nature of many of the deposits means that the samian cannot be used to refine the dating of the stratigraphic phases. The range suggested by the assemblage, however, presumably reflects the duration of occupation of the site.

The potters' stamps (Brenda Dickinson)
1. PATERCLV[SF], Dr 18/31 (Fig 9.13): Paterclvs ii of Central Gaul, Die 12a. 355/3076, Phase 3.3

This stamp appears to have been used only on dishes of Form 18/31, of Trajanic type, and cups of Form 27. Paterclvs ii is one of the potters who started his career at Les Martres-de-Veyre and ended it at Lezoux; this particular stamp has been found at Les Martres, but there is no evidence from the fabrics and glazes of the other vessels on which it occurs that its die was ever used at Lezoux. Site dating for this common stamp is sparse, but there is a burnt example in the London second fire deposits *c* AD 100-120.

2. [ ]MI, Dr 15/17 or 18, Southern Gaul. Potter not identified, Flavian. 88/1112, Phase 1.4

Catalogue of illustrated vessels (Fig 9)

For a full catalogue of decorated vessels see Appendix 2. Numbers refer to Figure 9 and are listed in order of production date.

1. (Cat no 19), La Graufesenque, Dr 37, rim, body and base sherds. The style is that of Germanus of La Graufesenque. Date: AD 70-85.
371/3036, 355/3078/3079/3083, Phase 3.3

2. (Cat no 7), La Graufesenque, Dr 29, body. Date: AD 75-85.
338/1268, Phase 1.3

3. (Cat no 6), La Graufesenque, Dr 29 or 37, body. Date: Flavian or Flavian/Trajanic.
230/1178, Phase 1.3

4. (Cat no 12), La Graufesenque, Dr 37, body. Date: AD 85-110.
57/3018, Phase 1:4

5. (Cat no 11), La Graufesenque, Dr 37, body. Date: AD 85-110.
057/3017, Phase 1.4

6. (Cat no 25), La Graufesenque, Dr 37, body. Date: Late Flavian or Trajanic.
031/1050, Phase 2/3

7. (Cat no 1), Les Martres-de-Veyre, Dr 37 rim. Potter X-13, Date: Trajanic.
256/1193, Phase 1.1

8. Cat no 14), Les Martres-de-Veyre, Dr 37. Potter X-13. Date: Trajanic.
079/1079, (Phase 1.4

9. (Cat no 15), Pre-export Lezoux, Dr 37, rim. Potter X-12. Date: AD 100-120.
371/1291, Phase 2.2

10. (Cat no 24), Lezoux, Dr 37, body. The work is that of the Sacer group, but perhaps has more in common with Attianus than other potters of this group. Date: AD 125-145.
533/1369, Phase 3.3

11. (Cat no 10), Lezoux, body/footring. Date: AD 125-150.
057/1061, Phase 1.4

12. (Cat no 8), Lezoux (fabric more orange than is normal), Dr 37, body. Sacer. Date: AD 125-150.
011/1039, Phase 1.4

Coarse Pottery (L Hird)

A total of 877 sherds (32kg) of fine and coarsewares was recovered from the site, most stratified (81.9%). The assemblage comprised 653 fragments of fine and coarsewares, 160 of amphora, and 64 of mortarium.

The pottery was recorded by context onto *proforma* sheets, using a fabric series to avoid repetition; sherds were recorded by weight, count, vessel type, rim diameter and percentage rim. The record sheets have been placed within the archive. Tables 2-4 provide a breakdown of the material by fabric and sherd count. Twenty-nine vessels are illustrated (Figs 10.1-29).

Fabric	1	2	3	4	5	6	7	8	9	10	11	12	13	14	15
Phase 1.1	2							1			7	13			
Phase 1.2	9				1			2			13	24	5		
Phase 1.3	5	1				1			2		12	9			
Phase 1.4	16	6	1	5	6	17	15	1			50	19			
Phase 1.5															
Phase 2.1												16			
Phase 2.2					1		3				11	4			
Phase 3.1	1		1		1					2	6	6			2
Phase 3.2															
Phase 3.3	3		4		7		1		2	5	61	35		3	
Phase 2/3	6	14						2	1		15	28			
Phase 4															
TOTAL	42	21	6	5	16	18	39	6	5	7	175	154	5	3	2

Table 2: Coarse/fine wares, quantities by phase/fabric/sherd count

Fabric	20	21	22	23	24	25	26
Phase 1.1	4						
Phase 1.2	45		1				
Phase 1.3	13						
Phase 1.4	30	4	5	4		1	8
Phase 1.5							
Phase 2.1							
Phase 2.2				1			
Phase 3.1	15						
Phase 3.2							
Phase 3.3	6				1		1
Phase 2/3	22						
Phase 4							
TOTAL	135	4	6	5	1	1	9

Table 3: Amphorae, quantities by phase/fabric/sherd count

Fabric	30	31	32	33	34	35	36	37	38
Phase 1.1	3						3		
Phase 1.2	3								
Phase 1.3	1	1	1						
Phase 1.4	6			1	1	1			
Phase 1.5									
Phase 2.1									
Phase 2.2									
Phase 3.1		3	19						2
Phase 3.2									
Phase 3.3	1	1	1				1	1	
Phase 2/3	3		1						
Phase 4									
TOTAL	17	5	22	1	1	1	4	1	2

Table 4: Mortaria, quantities by phase/fabric/sherd count

The pottery from Kirkham has all been to some extent adversely affected by soil conditions and the oxidised wares, in particular, have lost surfaces and become powdery. In many cases where the fabric originally bore a cream slip, it now remains only as a trace.

Coarse pottery fabric series

1. *Black Burnished Ware 1 (BB1). Williams 1977.*
This was present in all but Phase 2 (which produced little pot). All vessels represented are of early/mid second century date, and include Figure 10.7. BB1 first appears in the North in the AD 120s (Gillam 1976) and its appearance in Phase 1 suggests a Hadrianic date. It was also present in the earliest phase at the neighbouring site of Walton-le-Dale (Hird forthcoming b), unlike Ribchester (Hird forthcoming a) where it was absent in the two earliest phases.

2. *Fine-textured, soft, powdery, buff fabric with slightly paler outer surface.*

3. *Fine-textured, orange fabric with dark brown/black slip and rough-cast decoration. Gaulish. Anderson 1980.*
Only six sherds (including Fig 10.20) of this fabric were recovered, from Phases 1 and 3. This is believed (Anderson 1980) to be dated to the period c AD 80-130/5.

4. *Rough, grey fabric with large (1mm) white inclusions (?calcite). Appears hand-made.*
There are five sherds of this hand-made, possibly 'native'? fabric from Phase 1.4.

5. *Sandy, oxidised, orange fabric with cream slip.*
Oxidised wares (see also Fabrics 10 and 12) appear in all phases, and probably derive from several local sources including Wilderspool (eg Figs 10.1, 10.12, 10.17), which also provided a considerable number of mortaria. Wilderspool is believed to have begun production in the late first or early second century and its products are present in Phase 1 contexts.

6. *Granular-textured, sandy, buff fabric.*

7. *Rustic Ware. Sandy, pale grey fabric with rusticated decoration.*
In total, 39 sherds of rustic ware were recovered from the site, 35 of them from Phase 1 contexts. Rustic ware is conventionally dated to the period c AD 80-130 but, by the Hadrianic period, it is less common than in the late first/earlier second century; no rims were recovered which might have enabled the dating to be refined.

8. *Sandy, whitish-cream fabric.*

9. *Very fine-textured, creamy-white fabric.*

10. *Fine-textured, oxidised fabric with red particle inclusions.*

11. *Unidentified grey ware. Probably the product of more than one local source.*
Greywares were present in all but Phase 2, and were probably the products of more than one local source. They include little to suggest very local production, except that Fig.10.21 could be regarded as a slight 'second', although certainly usable.

12. *Unidentified oxidised ware. Probably the product of more than one local source.*

13. *Very fine-textured, white fabric with dark grey colour-coat. Rhineland product?*

14. *Terra Nigra. Grey fabric with light grey layer beneath surfaces, which are highly burnished. Rigby 1973.*
Three sherds of first century Terra Nigra were recovered from Phase 3.3, where they were without doubt residual

15. *Sandy, oxidised, orange fabric with grey core and mica-dusted outer surface.*
Only two sherds were recovered, both from Phase 3.1. Mica-dusting was a technique used particularly in the late first/early second century.

Amphora fabric series

20. *Sandy, rough, buff-grey fabric, often flaky. The usual fabric for South Spanish olive oil amphorae of Dressel 20, Peacock and Williams Class 25 (1986).*

21. *Self-coloured, fine-textured, bright orange fabric with sparse quartz sand and larger (up to 5mm) particles of quartz and reddish material. Gaulish?*

22. *Fine-textured, creamy-white fabric with small red inclusions.*

23. *Fine-textured, buff fabric with red inclusions and paler outer surface. Cadiz fabric. Peacock and Williams Class 17 (1986).*

53

24. *Granular-textured, self-coloured, creamy-white or pink fabric with pale pink core and occasional red particle inclusions. Gaulish?*

25. *Sandy, rough, pink fabric with paler outer surface. Gaulish?*

26. *Fine-textured, pink fabric with pinkish-buff outer surface and occasional red inclusions. Gaulish.*

Most of the amphora sherds from the site (135; 84%) were of South Spanish olive oil amphorae, Fabric 20, from Phases 1 and 3. There were no rims, but several handle fragments were present. Olive oil amphorae of Peacock and Williams Class 25 (1986) are common finds on sites from the first to the third centuries.

There were five sherds of another South Spanish fabric (Fabric 23) in Phases 1.4 and 2.2.. These sherds may be from vessels used to transport fish sauce, and date to the late first/early second century. The remaining sherds are of Gaulish wine amphorae and include Figure 10.15 and Figure 10.27.

Mortarium fabric series

30. *Fine-textured, sandy, bright orange fabric, sometimes with a grey core. Mixed trituration grit of red-brown, white and grey material. Wilderspool.*

31. *As Fabric 30 but with a cream slip. Wilderspool.*

32. *Granular-textured, cream or creamy-pink fabric with red inclusions. Verulamium region.*

33. *Fine-textured, cream fabric. Grey trituration grit.*

34. *Sandy, self-coloured, pale grey fabric with mixed, mostly grey grit.*

35. *Fine-textured, rather granular, pinkish-cream fabric with cream surfaces and small red inclusions. Trituration grit includes quartz.*

36. *Fine-textured, buff fabric, with trace of cream slip. Fabric includes quartz grit. Wilderspool?*

37. *Fine-textured, usually softish, white to brownish-cream fabric with quartz and flint inclusions. Trituration grit is mainly flint with occasional quartz and red-brown material. Gallia Belgica, including the Pas de Calais.*

38. *Granular-textured, slightly micaceous, cream fabric with mixed trituration grit of quartz, sandstone and red-brown material. South Carlton, Lincoln.*

Twenty-six (48%) of the mortaria sherds were Wilderspool products, which date to the period *c* AD 110-160 (Hartley and Webster 1973). These were present in Phases 1 and 3 (Figs 10.3, 10.5, 10.6, 10.16, 10.18). Sherds of Gallo-Belgic vessels, Fabric 37, occur residually in Phase 2/3 and in a modern context (Fig 10.28). Another source which provided mortaria to the North in the first century was the Verulamium region (Fabric 32) and there is a stamped vessel from this source, recovered from Phase 3.1, where it was clearly residual. The only other mortarium stamp (Fig 10.29), on a vessel of Fabric 38, was also from a modern context.

Dating

Dating of the coarse pottery from Kirkham suggests a very short-lived occupation beginning in the early/mid second century (Hadrianic) and not extending much, if at all, beyond the middle of the same century.

First century vessels are present, but all are of types which persist into the early years of the second century (ie Gallo-Belgic and Verulamium region mortaria, and Terra Nigra). A notable absentee among the repertoire of vessels present is the carinated, reeded rim bowl, which is typical of the late first/early second century and which is common at Ribchester (Hird forthcoming a) and other sites in the North. This form is also relatively infrequent at Walton-le-Dale (Hird forthcoming b).

The dated vessels from Phase 3 are all of early/mid second century date, not distinguishably later than the Phase 1 material.

Catalogue of illustrated coarsewares

1. Fabric 12, bowl. Very abraded. *cf* Wilderspool, Hartley and Webster 1973, fig 6.50, and Walton-le-Dale type 179 (Hird forthcoming b). *c* AD 110-160.
135, Phase 1.1

2. Fabric 5, flagon. Very abraded. Very little slip remains. Gillam 4 (1970). AD 90-130.
024, Phase 1.2

3. Fabric 30, mortarium. Wilderspool.
229, Phase 1.2

4. Fabric 1, jar.
338, Phase 1.3

5. Fabric 30, mortarium. Wilderspool.
230, Phase 1.3

6. Fabric 31, mortarium. Wilderspool.
005, Phase 1.3

7. Fabric 1, dish. Gillam 55 (1976). Early/mid second century.
057, Phase 1.4

8. Fabric 6, bowl. Base and rim sherds do not join.
079, Phase 1.4

9. Fabric 1, jar.
088, Phase 1.4

10. Fabric 11, beaker. *cf* Ribchester type 93 (Hird forthcoming a) where it occurs in a Phase 3 context. Second century onwards.
057; 070, Phase 1.4

11. Fabric 11, dish.
466, Phase 1.4

12. Fabric 12, flagon. Wilderspool (Hartley and Webster 1973, fig 2.3).
088, Phase 1.4

13. Fabric 12, two-handled flagon.
Context 057, Phase 1.4

14. Fabric 12, bowl/dish. *cf* Ribchester type 133 (Hird forthcoming a) where it occurs in reduced fabric from Ribblesdale Mill Phase 1. Second century onwards.
057, Phase 1.4

15. Fabric 21, amphora. Possibly Peacock and Williams Class 29 (1986).
057, Phase 1.4

16. Fabric 30, mortarium. Unusual rim form. Wilderspool.
057, Phase 1.4

17. Fabric 10, flagon. Wilderspool (Hartley and Webster 1973, fig 2.5).
219, Phase 3.1

18. Fabric 31, mortarium. Only a trace of cream slip remains. Trituration grit mostly quartz. Wilderspool.
355; 360; 371, Phase 3.1

19. Fabric 38, mortarium. South Carlton, Lincoln?
219, Phase 3.1

20. Fabric 3, beaker. Gaulish rough-cast. Anderson's North Gaulish fabric 1 (1980). AD 80-130/5.
533, Phase 3.3

21. Fabric 11, jar. *cf* Ribchester type 65 (Hird forthcoming a) where it occurs in Phase 3 contexts. Slight 'second'. Second century onwards.
371, Phase 3.3

22. Fabric 11, jar.
371, Phase 3.3

23. Fabric 11, jar.
371, Phase 3.3

24. Fabric 11, storage jar.
371, Phase 3.3

25. Fabric 11, jar. *cf* Ribchester type 62 (Hird forthcoming a) where it occurs in Phase 2. Second century onwards.
355, Phase 3.3

26. Fabric 11, lid.
355, Phase 3.3

27. Fabric 24, amphora. Peacock and Williams Class 27 (1986). Gaulish wine amphora.
355, Phase 3.3

28. Fabric 37, mortarium. Gallo-Belgic. Gillam 238 (1970). AD 60-100.
175, Modern

29. Fabric 38, mortarium. South Carlton, Lincoln. Stamped.
175, Modern

Post-Roman Pottery

A limited amount of medieval and post-medieval/modern pottery was recovered from the site. It is of little significance, in itself, but does allow the dating and recognition of disturbed and residual contexts. The presence and significance of late pottery within a context is noted in the main stratigraphic narrative. A catalogue appears in the archive.

The Coin (DCA Shotter)

Only one coin was recovered from the excavations:

> AE *As*, Vespasian   *RIC* 482   AD 71
>
> *Obv.* [IMP CAES VESPASIAN AVG COS] III
>
> *Rev.* [AEQVITAS] AVGVSTI SC
>
> 379/1349, Phase 2.2

(The coin is fragmentary, but was apparently little worn when lost).

Few other Roman coins have been recorded; Watkin (1883, 206) mentions three - an *aureus* of Vespasian and two *aes* - issues of Hadrian; these were found in the nineteenth century, evidently outside the fort-area. Watkin had no information on the types or condition of these coins. More recently (1994), a very worn *as* of Vespasian was reported to have been found near the railway-station. Thus, the coin from the excavations is the only one to which a precise date-of-issue can be assigned; in the light of current discussions regarding the dating of early Roman activity in north-west England (Shotter 1994), it is clearly of some significance that this coin was a little worn issue of AD 71.

Three other coin-finds from the area should be mentioned:

1) A hoard of *denarii* was found in Poulton Street in 1853, concealed in a small samian jar (Dechelette 67). This hoard, which is now in the Harris Museum at Preston, consisted of 35 *denarii* (from Tiberius to Balbinus) and a *semis* of Nero (Sutherland 1936, 316-320); it is possible that the group conceals more than a single hoard, since by the time that this hoard terminated – in AD 238 – the coin of Tiberius would have been officially demonetised – by a decree of the Emperor Trajan, in *c* AD 107, who recalled all pre-Neronian silver coins for melting down.

Between the time of its discovery (1853) and that of its assessment in the 1930s, the hoard had acquired six 'intruders' – one coin each of Octavian, Severus Alexander, Trajan Decius, and Honorius, and two of Gallienus. There is no indication of the source of these, nor whether they were in any way connected with Kirkham.

2) It appears that a hoard of radiates was found in the 1950s near to the railway-line at Treales. Two coins have been offered for examination - a radiate each of Gallienus (*RIC* 160) and of Tetricius (*RIC* 68), and it is said that others remain locally in private hands. It is worth noting that the County Record Office in Preston has a reference to a radiate of Gallienus (*RIC* 574) having been found at Treales in the 1920s.

3) A dispersed hoard of 17 *denarii* has been found at intervals in recent years at Naze Mount; the coins range in date from the Republic (Marcus Antonius) to the reign of Marcus Aurelius (AD 161–80).

The last two hoards are discussed in Shotter 1995 (50 and 52); the presence of these three hoards in the vicinity of the military site at Kirkham presumably points to nearby rural settlement operating at a reasonably prosperous level.

Copper Alloy

Five fragments of copper alloy were recovered, of which the button (2) from topsoil 3 and the two fragments of pipe (3) from 287 are clearly modern. The other two objects were both brooches. One (4) is fragmentary and little can be added, especially as it was unstratified. The other (1) (276, revetment footings, Phase 3.1) appears to be part of a Polden Hill-type brooch, probably of first or early second century date (Hattatt 1985). A catalogue appears in Appendix 2.

Ironwork

The ironwork from the site was not X-rayed, as the form of most of the fragments remained obvious despite corrosion. Thus, the only dimension given in Appendix 2 is an overall length, including corrosion products, intended simply to convey an impression of size.

Ten of the twelve fragments appeared to derive from nails; they appear evenly spread across the phases, but that (12) from 451 (Modern) is probably modern in date. The two other fragments both derive from Phase 3.3 contexts. That from the last fills of outwork ditch (533) is of little interest, a featureless fragment of strip (7). However, that from 355 (fill of ditch 354) is a large U-shaped hook or shackle (6) which might derive from a cart or other wheeled transport. A catalogue appears in Appendix 2.

Lead

There was nothing of relevance within the assemblage; a catalogue appears in Appendix 2.

Glass

A total of 24 fragments of glass was recovered from 16 contexts. Most were very small and, with one exception (2), the Roman glass vessel fragments were all natural blue-green (3, 7, 8, 10, 11, 14-17). All probably derived from square mould-blown storage bottles of common type, Isings 50 (1957), dating largely to the first and second centuries but, since they are very robust, often surviving into the third.

The single fragment of colourless glass (2) from 209 (fill of hollow 135, Phase 1.1), was a small cup base subsequently grozed to form a counter or tally. Such cups (Isings 85, 1957) are also a common type, dating mainly to the second century.

Three of the vessel fragments (12, 13, 18) were clearly post-medieval, with a fourth fragment (14), greenish bubbly window glass from context 278 (Modern), probably eighteenth century in date. All four fragments reinforce the air of late disturbance on the site.

There were also two beads, both from disturbed contexts, but both probably Roman, one (6), a small dark blue globular bead from 007 (fill of ditch 006, Phase 1.3), the other a small and poorly-made melon bead from cobble surface 277 (Phase 3). Neither can be closely dated, but, like most other finds from the site, they can be placed in the first to early third centuries.

Finally, three fragments of typical matte-glossy Roman window glass (1, 4) were also noted, from fills 209 (hollow 135, Phase 1.1) and 136 (ditch 052, Phase 1.2). These, also, are assigned a first-to-second century date but, like the storage vessels, such material often survives into the third century. A catalogue appears in Appendix 2.

Industrial Residues and Burnt Clay

Only a small amount of industrial residue was recovered, comprising isolated fragments of vitrified hearth lining and tiny amounts of what was probably smithing debris. The suggestion of a hearth amongst the somewhat disparate features associated with the extramural area (429 and associated features, Phase 2/3) might be reinforced by the slightly larger assemblage of industrial debris from that phase. Otherwise the amount of evidence is so small that it is only possible to state that some high temperature process, possibly blacksmithing, took place in the vicinity of the site at some time, probably during the Roman period.

In total, 102 small fragments of incidentally burnt clay were recovered, none retaining any indication of their original purpose or structure, although several appeared to have been fired to a very high temperature. It is thus likely that most, if not all, of the burnt clay derived from hearths or other structures associated with high temperature industrial process. A catalogue appears in the archive.

Tile and Brick

Almost 300 small fragments of brick and tile were recovered, most apparently Roman in date, although it is not always easy to differentiate between Roman and medieval examples. Due to the fragmentary nature of the assemblage the material was subjected to a rapid scan, noting the presence of distinctive tile and brick forms, such as roof tile (*imbrex* and *tegula*) and box flue tiles from hypocaust systems. As might be expected from such small fragments, few examples of distinctive tile types could be identified with confidence, although they were noted in several contexts. In general tile and brick was present only in small quantities in any particular context, although there was a peak in contexts associated with the extramural area, characterised as extended periods of general activity, without doubt including the demolition and renewal of buildings, which would have generated amounts of broken brick and tile. The presence of roof tiles and hypocaust flue tiles suggests that some, at least, of the buildings in the vicinity were of Roman type, and of reasonably high status. Earlier reports raised the possibility of a bath house in close proximity (Singleton 1980), and the assemblage could well have derived from such a building. A catalogue appears in the archive.

Stone

One of the three fragments of stone recovered is likely to be unmodified, while a second, a whetstone, derives from a modern context. The struck flint, from fill 410 (ditch 220, Phase 3.1), is likely to be residual prehistoric, but there is no reason why it could not be an *ad hoc* strike-a-light. Fragments of flint are found with relative frequency on Roman sites. A catalogue appears in the archive.

Leather

The two small fragments of leather, although well-preserved, can add little to an interpretation of activity on the site. Neither is of particularly diagnostic form, although that from ditch fill 338 (Phase 1.3) appears to be part of a narrow beaded seam (1). Seams like this are often associated with the gabled ends of military tents, but this particular example seems rather too insubstantial for such a position and must have derived from something smaller, perhaps saddlery. The second fragment (2), a small piece of seamed sheet leather, clearly derived from a sewn composite object.

Wood

Extensive waterlogging led to the excellent preservation of wood within some of the ditch fills of Phases 1 and 3. The entire assemblage, a total of 144 fragments, was retained and examined during post-excavation as the amount and character of the group (largely artefacts) justified total retrieval rather than sampling. The material was recorded using the system developed for the substantial assemblage of wood from Ribchester (see Howard-Davis forthcoming) based on that of MoLAS (Milne 1982).

A single object, the *pilum muralis*, has been conserved and, of the remainder, most is retained without conservation, prior experience demonstrating that careful packing in heat-sealed, airtight, 'customised' polythene wrappings significantly prolongs the life of unconserved waterlogged wood.

The assemblage divides clearly into two: scrap and waste wood, both modified and unmodified, and wooden artefacts, almost exclusively tent pegs. No systematic attempt at species identification was attempted, although most is likely to be oak.

Scrap and Waste Wood
Scrap and waste wood is present in small quantities in ditch fills associated with Phases 1 and 3 and from pit and gully fills in the extramural area (Phase 2/3). Much of this wood is unmodified, either small diameter roundwood, or larger trunks, in one case up to 200mm in diameter. No evidence for woodland management was noted amongst this very small group.

A small group of fragments from ditch fill 332 (Phase 3.1) may be primary conversion waste, suggesting that, even relatively late in the life of the complex, some timber conversion was undertaken on, or near, the site. Other riven but otherwise unmodified wood might also fall into this category.

Little can be said of techniques employed by Roman woodworkers on the site. Where determined, plank-sized fragments were radially converted and adze dressed, also the main techniques employed in timber buildings at Ribchester (Howard-Davis forthcoming). There they were thought to suggest a native or non-Roman element amongst the woodworkers.

Only small and obviously discarded (usually heavily burnt) fragments of timber were recovered, but there was enough ostensibly structural wood (such as planking) to draw the inference of timber buildings on the site, especially in Phase 1, although they might well have been of a temporary nature (perhaps even prefabricated?). No diagnostic woodworking debris, for example the distinctive chips generated by axe or adze work, or the blocks created by cutting joints, was noted.

It is, perhaps, a little puzzling that no wooden corduroy was encountered beneath the earthen rampart core of the Phase 3 ramparts, especially as the surrounding layers were extensively waterlogged. The use of timber foundations for such structures appears to have been more-or-less standard practice (see, for instance, Ribchester, Buxton and Howard-Davis forthcoming, for a local example) and the absence of such a structure at Kirkham may be of significance.

Tent Pegs
Around 50 notched pegs, of the kind normally described as tent pegs, were recorded. It proved difficult to establish an exact number as many were fragmentary and on occasion it is possible that several non-joining fragments may have derived from the same peg.

Most of the pegs appeared to be oak, usually, but not always, radially split. The split billet was subsequently shaped with a number of axe blows, giving a trapezoidal-sectioned head and triangular-sectioned point, slightly bevelled to give it a blade-like appearance. The heads of most examples from this group were trimmed, almost to a point. Although the method used to form the notch was similar in all cases (a slanting blow running inwards from the pointed end to within 100mm of the top, and severed by a second blow parallel to the top of the peg, making the notch effectively a right-angled triangle) the location of the notch and the depth and angle of the first cut was rather more variable than observed elsewhere (eg Ribchester, Howard-Davis forthcoming). The notch represents an obvious point of weakness where the pegs were most likely to break.

The length of individual pegs varied considerably but falls broadly into two groups, those of 0.35m or less, and those over 0.55m, suggesting that two sizes were required. The same approximate division can be seen within the larger, broadly contemporary assemblage of pegs from Ribchester (op cit). A single, unusually large peg, almost 1m in length, must have served some specific purpose. Presumably the pegs were used for both guy ropes and to pin the bottoms of the tents to the ground (van Driel Murray 1990).

These pegs have always been identified as tent pegs, largely on the basis of their resemblance to modern examples, and it is more than likely that they were often used for this purpose; it would, however, seem folly to suggest that such pegs were used solely for this function. They could, undoubtedly, have been put to numerous uses. The fact that this group appears to have been deposited as one, and that most have been damaged by use, might suggest that they were tent pegs, all used together, perhaps discarded when one or more tents were pitched or struck.

The pilum muralis
The only other object associated with the tent pegs was a long, carefully made stave of oak, identified as a *pilum muralis* (Buxton and Howard-Davis 1994) . This is presented here in summary only (Fig 11).

It is in essence an axe-dressed, square-sectioned, double-pointed stave about 1.2m long with a bulbous handgrip carved about one third of the way down its length. Although undoubtedly used in large quantities, such objects rarely survive, and fewer than ten examples are known from this country. The

Kirkham example closely resembles those illustrated by Bennett (1982, 201, A-E) from Great Chesters, Castleshaw, Saalburg and Welzheim, all of which have bulbous hand grips, rather than the example from Oberaden illustrated in Bishop and Coulston (1993, fig 63.1).

Vegetius (Book I, 24) describes 'fixed stakes of very strong wood, which soldiers are accustomed to carry with them', presumably similar to the example from Kirkham, although the exact function of these double-pointed stakes is still a matter for speculation (Gilliver 1993). It is, however, worth noting that this example, like that from Great Chesters, derives from the fill of a defensive ditch (fill 216, Phase 3.2), perhaps linking it with the fortifications.

No other recognisable artefacts were recovered, a catalogue appears in Appendix 2.

Animal Bone (LJ Gidney)

Very little animal bone was found during the excavation, and most proved unidentifiable. Of that recovered, most was burnt, a significant factor in its preservation; the ratio of burnt to unburnt fragments was 4:1. Most fragments were from the earliest military establishment (Phase 1). Only three species could be identified: cattle, sheep/goat, and dog.

The most frequently surviving remains of cattle were fragments of teeth (five items), of which only enamel survived. Phase 3.3 produced part of the proximal shaft of a femur, in a reasonable state of preservation, with marks of canid gnawing. The unphased modern material included a patella in poor condition which, from its size, is probably of recent origin.

The single sheep/goat bone from Phase 1.2 was a distal tibia with the epiphysis fused, and had survived only by being burnt. The isolated dog bone from Phase 3.3 was an ulna shaft, with a notch in the distal shaft which may have been human handiwork.

The most interesting find was part of a dog skeleton from fill 371 of ditch 354 (Phase 3.3), associated with the final phase of the fort. This animal was represented by the skull, both mandibles, part of one scapula, both humeri, both radii, both ulnae, four thoracic vertebrae, five lumbar vertebrae and 16 ribs. The permanent dentition was present and all the epiphysial ends were fused, indicating that the animal was over 18 months old (Sisson and Grossman 1975) and, since the sutures on the skull were not clearly visible and there was wear on the teeth, the animal was probably elderly at death. Both the humeri and radii and one ulna were sufficiently intact for the length to be measured. As can be seen from Table 5, the paired elements were not totally symmetrical.

Skull I	183
II	98.3
III	94.3
IV	94
IX	89.2
XI	67.5
XV	74.4
Cephalic Index	51.3
Snout Index	51.5

	Long bone lengths	Estimated shoulder height
Humerus	117.3	375mm
Humerus	118.3	379mm
Radius (L)	112	375mm
Radius (R)	109.4	367mm
Ulna (R)	130.6	369mm
Humerus and Radius (L)	229.3	374mm
Humerus and Radius (R)	227.7	371mm

Table 5: Measurements of dog skeleton in mm (after Harcourt 1974)

In particular, the left radius and ulna were considerably more bowed than the right, suggesting that the elbow on this side may have been more protuberant in life. These bones indicated that the animal was about 0.37m tall to the shoulder, using the factors given by Harcourt (1974). All the measurements fall within the lower end of the range for Romano-British dog bones established by Harcourt, but are not among the most diminutive known. Although the animal was not very tall, the bones are robust, suggesting that it was of stocky build, and not dissimilar to animals at the nearby fort of Ribchester (Stallibrass forthcoming). The type of animal may be visualised from some Romano-British figurines of dogs, for example the bronze of a short legged, long-snouted dog from Canterbury (Green 1992, fig 8.1) and the 'Aberdeen terrier' from Coventina's well at Carrawburgh (Toynbee 1962, plate 62). The absence of the entire hindquarters, all the cervical vertebrae, and all the metacarpals and phalanges suggests that this is not a primary burial and that these remains may have been unwittingly incorporated in the material used to fill this ditch. The excellent preservation of this find emphasises the absence of the general bone food refuse that is expected in association with Roman forts. A catalogue appears in Appendix 2.

Plant and Invertebrate Remains (J Carrott, A Hall, M Issitt, H Kenward, F Large, and B McKenna)

A series of samples of deposits was submitted for analysis of their content of plant and invertebrate remains. The samples came from 22 contexts, almost all representing features associated with the Roman stone fort, and mainly the fills of linear cuts interpreted as ditches. The analyses were carried out within a restricted budget, which placed constraints on the approach which could be taken.

Practical methods
Each sample was represented by between one and five 10l tubs of sediment (there were 48 in total; see Table 8 (Appendix 2)). In order to avoid confusion, where there was more than one tub each was assigned a unique sample number by adding 01, 02, etc, to the original number. The contents of all tubs were inspected in the laboratory and a description of their lithology recorded using a standard *pro forma*. At this stage, the samples were prioritised for further analysis.

Sub-samples of 1kg were taken from 21 of the samples for extraction of macrofossil remains, following procedures of Kenward *et al* (1980; 1986). In some cases, where 'waterlogged' organic remains were thought to be sparse or lacking, the 'light' fraction was recovered by a washover and paraffin flotation was not undertaken. Work on macro-invertebrates proceeded further by an initial assessment and prioritisation and then by scan-recording (*sensu* Kenward 1992) of selected material. Eleven of the selected samples (Table 8) were also examined for the eggs of parasitic nematodes using the methods of Dainton (1992).

Plant remains were recorded (using a semi-quantitative four-point scale of abundance) from the residues, either directly (by scanning, *sensu* Hall and Kenward 1990) or from selected material. The flots and washovers were also checked for plant remains. Components of the residues other than identifiable plant macrofossils were recorded during sorting/scanning, and a selection of insect remains which had not been extracted from the residues by paraffin flotation was identified.

For a few samples, all the remaining sediment (apart from a voucher) was 'bulk-sieved' to 1mm (with a 500 washover), the residue being sorted when dry for artefacts and larger plant remains.

Interpretative methods
For plant and insect macrofossils, the approach to interpretation followed that used by Hall and Kenward (1990). Thus, the lists of plant taxa were subjected to an analysis which uses a series of 'ecological' and 'use' groups. The assemblages of adult beetles and bugs were examined for their 'community structure' using the index of diversity, alpha, of Fisher *et al* (1943), regarded here as indicative of the degree of heterogeneity of origin of the death assemblage. It should be noted that the 'outdoor' component referred to below has a significance beyond the identification of assemblages as having formed inside or outside buildings. Statements concerning statistics of insect assemblages are relative to the distribution of values seen in a very large number of groups from archaeological occupation sites of many kinds.

Results
The samples were all essentially silts and clays with a varying proportion of organic matter, sometimes coarse detritus in lenses but more generally present as fine detritus or amorphous humic material distributed through the matrix.

Plant remains were recorded from 21 subsamples representing 17 contexts. A third of the sub-samples were devoid of identifiable remains; for the remaining sub-samples, the minimum number of taxa ranged from two to 44 (the mean being 22). Preservation was almost exclusively by anoxic 'waterlogging', and the quality of preservation varied quite considerably. Apart from charcoal, almost no charred plant remains were recorded, even from the bulk-sieved sub-samples. There were certainly no charred cereal remains, evidence for this group of plants being present only in the form of 'waterlogged' wheat/rye 'bran' from five subsamples from three contexts and traces of ?wheat chaff fragments from two contexts. Two of the 'squashes' examined for parasite eggs produced traces of *Trichuris* sp.

Eight of the sub-samples were barren of macro-invertebrates or contained only insignificant traces. A further eight, representing seven contexts, gave small groups of very limited interpretative significance individually, but of some value in the context of the material from the site as a whole. Six sub-samples from four contexts gave more substantial assemblages which were scan-recorded. One of the sub-samples giving a small assemblage contained fragments of the stag beetle *Lucanus cervus* (*see* Appendix 2, Table 7) and, in an attempt to recover more specimens, a further, much larger sub-sample was processed, the insect remains in it being rapid scan-recorded (*sensu* Kenward 1992). All these remains were preserved by anoxic waterlogging, the condition of the fossils ranging from 'average' to 'poor' by comparison with typical material from occupation sites with such preservation.

The results of the investigations have been incorporated into the stratigraphic text. A full list of taxa recorded is given in Appendix 2 (Tables 6 and 7). Table 8 (Appendix 2) gives a list of the samples for which some action was taken.

Discussion
Excavation of the site was undertaken by means of a large number of trenches, many of which were machine excavated; safety constraints often precluded detailed recording. Therefore the deposits were thinly sampled and there were certainly some cases (eg fill 353) where it was not possible to sample an overtly organic deposit.

Although most of the samples examined (and all of those with an appreciable fossil content) came from the fills of ditches, the quantity of 'waterlogged' biological remains and the quality of their preservation were very varied, some sub-samples being effectively barren and others rich in remains, some giving good preservation and others poor. Those sub-samples for which interpretatively large enough assemblages of plant and invertebrate remains were recorded showed a broad consistency, with evidence for dung, probably sometimes in the form of stable manure, and vegetation favoured by nutrient enrichment. Several of the samples contained small numbers of insects likely to have originated in animal (probably horse) feed, but gave little evidence of stable manure proper. Rather, there were strong hints of deposition where there was dung on ground surfaces. It is postulated that a few 'indoor' species of this kind were introduced via dung deposited in the open by animals fed, probably indoors, on hay and cereals.

Some other Roman sites for which plant and insect macrofossils have been investigated have produced evidence of large-scale disposal of what has been interpreted as stable manure, for example Ribchester, Lancashire (Large *et al* 1994), Lancaster, Lancashire (Wilson 1988), Papcastle, Cumbria (Kenward and Allison 1995) and Carlisle (Allison *et al* 1991; Allison and Kenward in press; Kenward *et al* 1991; Kenward, Allison *et al* 1992; Kenward, Dainton *et al* 1992a; b). For the Roman fort at Ribchester, it was remarked that 'the importance of stable manure at a military site such as a fort is perhaps hardly surprising. What is rather more unexpected is the rarity of evidence of other kinds of wastes detectable by insect remains. It appears that the site was kept pretty much clear of other wastes and of more than a thin vegetation cover for most of the period represented'. The site at Kirkham shows similar evidence but with less emphasis on the disposal of stable manure and more evidence for local vegetation (whether in or beside the ditches, or represented by imported turves). Papcastle, too, seems to have been very similar. Roman forts in the North seem, as perhaps might be predicted, to have had a somewhat uniform character with a discipline in waste disposal, but so much horse manure was generated that it inevitably left detectable evidence in the ground. Alternatively, or perhaps as well, horse dung was not seen as especially offensive (again, perhaps a product of familiarity or inevitability?), as suggested by Hall and Kenward (1990, 404).

Another probable component of at least some of the deposits examined from this site was turf, most of it probably from an area with acid soils, such as heathland or moorland. This interpretation rests largely on the botanical evidence but there were substantial numbers of insects consistent with it from the samples as a whole. None of the insects gave incontrovertible evidence of heathland or heather-dominated moorland, however, although most records for *Helophorus tuberculatus* are for such places.

Some of the deposits contained what appeared to be ash and/or burnt soil: in the fills of features of Phase 1.4 (79, 160, 462), as well as pit fill 279, and perhaps also fill 431 of a hollow associated with industrial activity (Phase 2/3). Some material which may have been 'baked' peat was recorded in pit fill 222 (Phase 2.2). This

?peat seems to have dried completely without being burnt, either by being near a fire or, perhaps, through dehydration in a dry atmosphere. It is possible that it was imported as fuel or stable litter, but it may equally well have originated in humus-rich turf, such as a moor soil brought to the site for construction.

The analyses produced little evidence of waste disposal directly into the features other than the deposition of quite large quantities of ash (although this may have found its way into the deposits indirectly via surface material). Layer 443 (Phase 2/3), however, clearly contained some possible industrial residue in the form of massive concretions. There is certainly no reason to suppose that waste from food preparation, or human faeces, were deliberately disposed of in the cut features. Evidence for foodplants is very sparse at this site; apart from a few fig seeds (and these are remarkably resistant to decay) and some wheat/rye 'bran' (which, as has been noted, may have been from animal feed), the only plant remains likely to have been eaten were rare seeds of blackberry, raspberry and elderberry, all easily arriving in other ways. Only two of the samples examined gave any eggs of intestinal parasites and these may not have originated in humans or may have entered the deposits indirectly via a variety of routes.

Other waste from human domestic occupation was also absent. The 'domestic' and stored products insects are all likely to have been associated with stabling and animal feed, and the single human flea is inadequate evidence for the incorporation of material from dwellings.

The replicate samples from single contexts were often rather different in lithology and there was much heterogeneity within some of the samples. This was reflected to some extent in the biota, but conclusions drawn from the assemblages were essentially consistent. A likely origin for much of the fills is surface 'soil' from the immediate surroundings, bringing with it a variety of sediment types, ranging from essentially mineral subsoil through humus- (and fossil-) rich surface layers to dung or stable manure deposited on them.

Notable insect records
Some of the records of beetles from this site are sufficiently interesting and unusual to deserve further comment. The remains of the stag beetle *Lucanus cervus* from ditch 218 (fill 330 Phase 3.2) have been discussed in Chapter 5, Phase 3.2. The small chafer beetle *Hoplia philanthus*, many of the remains distinguished by the characteristic and beautiful oval metallic scales, was recorded from six sub-samples representing three contexts (216, 330, 425). Remains suspected to have been of *H philanthus* have occasionally been noted from other Roman sites, in particular Carlisle, but this is the first material seen by the authors to have been sufficiently well preserved for a confident determination (one specimen from Old Grapes Lane A, Carlisle (Kenward, Allison *et al* 1992) can now be definitely identified by comparison with the Kirkham material). *H philanthus* is a root-feeder in the larval stage, the adults occurring in May to July, reportedly sometimes in quite large numbers locally (Jessop 1986, 29). The occurrence of *H. philanthus* is interesting in relation to the very frequent records of another small and supposedly locally abundant chafer, *Phyllopertha horticola*. It has been postulated that *P horticola* was a common component of background fauna but also likely to be imported in turf or cut vegetation (Kenward, Allison *et al* 1992, 8). Both chafers may have arrived at sites in these ways, or even have been accidentally eaten by livestock grazing on the turf in which the beetles pass their immature stages.

The specimen of terrestrial 'water beetle', *Helophorus tuberculatus* (Hansen 1987, 102), which appears to be rare in Britain at the present day (Balfour-Browne 1958, 95; Kenward 1976; Booth 1981), from ditch 056 (425, Phase 1.4) is also of note. The beetle is known from Roman deposits at Ribchester (Large *et al* 1994), Carlisle (Goodwin *et al* 1991, 23; Allison and Kenward in press; Kenward 1984;

65

Kenward, Allison *et al* 1992) and York (Kenward 1988; Hall and Kenward 1990). The consistency of occurrence of *H tuberculatus* in small numbers in archaeological deposits remains enigmatic, although it must be suspected that it was very much more common in the past than it seems to be now.

CHAPTER 8
DISCUSSION

Although its existence had been established for some time, very little was known of the Roman fort at Kirkham until these excavations; a search of the literature (Hodgkinson 1993) produces only a few passing references by antiquarian writers and, even in more recent times, work has been confined to the good offices of local enthusiasts, who have not always been in a position to publish, and who had only the sketchiest framework upon which to hang their researches.

These excavations have provided the first real opportunity to remedy this lack of knowledge. The sparseness of early work has meant that academic objectives outlined for the programme of excavation were couched in the broadest terms: to confirm the presence of a Roman military (or otherwise) establishment and to establish its chronological succession, thereby offering a framework for the future consideration of evidence from the site and the locality. To an extent the information gained from the site has been physically circumscribed by the areas available for excavation. This proved less of a hindrance than it might have, although inevitably the interior of the main, second century fort lay beyond the bounds of the excavation, beneath gardens and housing; the fact that the stone-revetted rampart of this fort lay directly below a modern land division may reflect the fossilisation of that boundary at an early date.

Despite the broad remit, there is little doubt that this programme of excavation more than achieved its academic aims, not only confirming the existence of a substantial, conventional Roman fort, but illustrating even quite transient activities on the site over the best part of a century. A parallel programme of finds and environmental study has helped to establish the contemporary local environment and, to a degree, the lifestyle and cultural preferences of those inhabiting the various structures on the site during that period.

Comparison with recent work (much of it yet to be published) at other Roman sites in the area, including Walton-le-Dale and Ribchester further to the east on the line of the River Ribble, and Lancaster and Carlisle to the north, has not only allowed Kirkham to be set within the landscape and contemporary events of the late first and second centuries AD, but has also allowed further refinement in the ongoing re-assessment of the period of Roman conquest in the North West during the AD 70s.

The Development of the Site

It has proved possible to define three distinct phases of Roman military activity on the site. A succession of temporary camps (Phase 1) was followed in turn by a signal station/fortlet (Phase 2) and a conventional stone-walled fort (Phase 3). These followed a loose chronological progression (there may have been a substantial overlap between Phases 1 and 2) as well as a rather more nebulous, low-level, indication of activity beyond the confines of the military establishment which may well have lasted through the whole period and, indeed, have endured beyond the demise of the fort, into the third century, or later.

Extensive recent environmental research (Middleton *et al* 1995) has enabled a fairly confident picture to be drawn of the conditions prevalent over the Fylde during the late Iron Age. Much of the area lay beneath extensive raised bogs, many of which had been in existence since the Neolithic or earlier. There is very little archaeological evidence for the existence or activities of Iron Age groups in the area (Haselgrove 1996, 61) except to note that during the period, land clearance and the beginnings of cereal cultivation can be seen in the palaeoenvironmental record (Wells *et al* 1997) suggesting that, although the Iron Age population might have been sparse and dispersed, the area was settled.

Sea-level studies (Tooley 1980) have also suggested that the coastline might have differed substantially to that seen today; most significantly, it seems likely that the sea-marsh at Freckleton Naze may, around that time, have been a significant embayment, bringing tidal water much closer to Kirkham than at present. Again, prehistoric groups are likely to have exploited the rich resources of the Ribble estuary.

It seems likely that the Iron Age population of the area was sparse and socially under-developed, especially when compared with late Iron Age societies in the South. There is, as yet, nothing to suggest that the long narrow moraine upon which the Roman site at Kirkham stands was either cleared or inhabited prior to the arrival of the Romans. Possible evidence for tree root systems, in the form of amorphous, meandering features pre-dating the earliest obviously Roman ditches, might even imply that the site was still wooded when the Romans arrived.

It has been suggested (Phase 1) that the earliest Roman activity is represented by a series of three temporary camps defined by relatively insubstantial, but clearly military, ditches, which appear superimposed and re-cut, suggesting periods during which they were abandoned or unused. These ditches are difficult to date as many of the fills were disturbed in antiquity or had been deliberately backfilled with midden waste from elsewhere, a not unsurprising practice which is becoming increasingly recognised in the archaeological record, as at Ribchester (Buxton and Howard-Davis forthcoming) or Dorchester (Woodward *et al* 1993) on both military and civilian sites. Dating evidence from the coarse pottery and the samian ware does not entirely agree, although both suggest a relatively long period during which these ditches filled. Coarsewares suggest a start date for Phase 1 in the early years of the second century (nothing ostensibly pre-Hadrianic) whilst the high proportion of South Gaulish samian (produced for export during the first century), which includes, albeit late, examples of vessel forms which went out of production by *c* AD 85, suggests an earlier date for the inception of Roman activity, in the late AD 70s or early 80s. Alongside this, a little worn coin of Vespasian, dated to AD 71, and presumably lost fairly soon afterwards, has led Shotter to suggest (*see* Chapter 7: The Coin, 54) an Agricolan (or even earlier) origin for the Roman presence at Kirkham (Shotter 1997, 14).

It is unlikely that any of these successive camps was in use for an extended period, although the presence of some internal features, such as a possible timber-lined latrine from Phase 1.4, might suggest that some periods of occupation were long enough to warrant permanent or semi-permanent structures.

The ditches appear to represent a stratigraphic and spatial succession, with the southernmost ditch probably earliest (Phase 1.2) and the northernmost latest (Phase 1.4). There also appears to have been a change of environment from the freshly dug easily eroded first ditch, through to the water-filled, grass-covered last, probably abandoned for some time before being deliberately backfilled and levelled.

The fills of the Phase 1.2 ditch appear to represent a cyclic or sporadic erosion, possibly the result of repeated superficial clearance of the ditch edges, preventing the development of vegetation, or perhaps of rain washing unconsolidated upcast from the accompanying bank back into the ditch; the suggestion, however ephemeral, of a retaining palisade revetting such a bank might add weight to the latter. Palaeoenvironmental evidence from Phase 1.3 suggests open grassland around, and even perhaps over, the defences, with evidence for grazing animals (horses) alongside stable waste and animal feed. Salt-marsh plants amongst the recorded flora might suggest that the animals were allowed to forage over a relatively wide area or, as might seem more likely with horses, that they were confined, hobbled or tethered, and fodder brought in from a number of sources, including the Ribble estuary and/or the Fylde Coast; a third inference might see horses ridden to the estuary and left to graze whilst their riders carried out their duties, a tempting if insubstantial first link between Kirkham and the coast.

The Punic ditch (Phase 1.4) provides evidence for intermittent standing water, presumably indicating that it stood open for a number of seasons, perhaps abandoned to decay for a fairly long period, whilst activity was focused elsewhere. Alongside this, environmental evidence again points towards grazing animals in the immediate vicinity, strongly suggesting pasture, presumably including the overgrown sides of the ditches; as in Phase 1.3, it seems likely that the animals were housed and fed elsewhere as there is a strong element of stored grain amongst the assemblage (wheat/rye), but clearly they were also turned out to graze, perhaps suggesting a fairly secure environment where there was little risk of their loss.

In Phase 1.4 there is the first hint of contact with the indigenous population, as a small amount of hand-made pottery appears in the assemblage, characterised by Hird (Fabric 4: Chapter 7, 51) as 'possibly native' and resembling (M Fletcher, pers comm) Iron Age or native types further south, at sites such as Castle Steads, Bury. Interestingly it appeared in ditch fills, suggesting not that the indigenous population was in direct contact with the fort, but that they were on site after the last temporary camp was abandoned, perhaps using the ditch as a casual repository for waste including ash and fragmentary burnt bone (domestic rubbish?), but before the area was levelled and backfilled early in the lifetime of the stone fort. The first evidence of arable farming comes from the same fills, with weeds of cultivation recorded within the palaeoenvironmental samples.

It is clear, however, that the site was never entirely abandoned by the Romans. The amount of Roman artefacts, mainly pottery, from ditch fills suggests a continuing presence and it is tempting to see a substantial overlap between the temporary camps and the small signal station/fortlet further up hill to the east (Phase 2).

It has already been suggested that the first, if transient, occupation of the site could have been Agricolan or earlier, a temporary camp to accommodate troops landed from the sea on their way to join the main northwards push of his northern campaigns. Pragmatism would suggest that the main land routes used in the Roman period would have crossed the drier land to the east of West Lancashire and the Fylde. If the strategic consideration of the lowest point of the Ribble is removed, then it must be suggested that not only Kirkham's foundation, but also its continued existence, looked to the sea, for otherwise there seems no reason for the erection of a fort in an area little settled by, and presumably of little value to, the Romans. If, as seems probable, Kirkham provided a convenient sea landing for the transhipment of goods and troops inland via the Ribble to Ribchester and points north and east, about a day's sail from the Dee and Chester (T Strickland, pers comm), but had little other strategic value, it would have seemed most sensible to erect a defended fortlet and signalling station with only a small permanent garrison, and simply to re-build or refurbish temporary camps as troop movement dictated.

No extramural settlement appears to have grown up around the fortlet during this phase. It is quite possible, however, that local families were drawn in, partly through curiosity, partly to exploit the growing cleared area, as the fortlet drew on local woodland for building material and fuel, using the land as grazing, and possibly for more settled cultivation. Of course, it is not impossible that a small and isolated garrison may well have been expected to look in part to its own resources for bulk provisions, perhaps encouraging the growth of cash crops locally, or raising its own cereals to supplement supplies brought in by land and sea.

Phase 2 activity cannot be securely dated, and there is reason to believe that there was a substantial overlap with Phase 1. This phase is represented by the erection of a small (40m side) ditched and defended enclosure with defensive outworks. There is also slight but convincing evidence for substantial timber buildings within the enclosure, possibly a tower. It obviously remained in existence for some time, long enough for the defences to have partially silted up and to have required renewal, first by a re-cut of the original line, and then possibly complete replacement with a large wooden palisade, a reasonable modification if the fortlet served partly as entrepot.

If the temporary camps (Phase 1) and the fortlet (Phase 2) were indeed broadly contemporary, then the small size of the establishment might, in part, account for the continued tendency to graze horses immediately outside the defences. This practice has been noted elsewhere (Dixon and Southern 1992, 196; Buxton and Howard-Davis forthcoming) although here, unlike Ribchester, there does not appear to have been any appreciable build-up of stable waste and dung heaps. Perhaps the more rural setting and the smaller garrison (not necessarily cavalry) meant that the disposal problem from stables was less, with nearby farms welcoming supplementary fertiliser, especially if their presence was in part due to the encouragement of the fort authorities.

Palaeoenvironmental evidence from the fills of the first Phase 2 ditch suggests trampled ground with poor drainage, perhaps representing the immediate surrounds, trampled by grazing animals and the day-to-day commerce of the fortlet, or alternatively the trampled backfill of the first ditch as the later palisade was erected. Numerous fragments of very dry, possibly baked, peaty material were encountered within these fills, as well as evidence of an element of acid-loving flora, suggesting the presence of peat, perhaps imported and dried for use as a fuel.

Although disparate, there were several outlying features associated with this phase. One may well have provided secondary defence, a ditch (and bank?) covering the entrance to the enclosure. Others, mainly pits, some of which may have been latrines or cesspits, lay within the area covered by the original temporary camps, often cutting earlier features, and suggesting an element of continuity in function.

Phase 2 is characterised by a marked lack of finds: a single coin and a few fragments of coarseware vessel. This seems to a degree puzzling, although perhaps it is reasonable to suggest that the inhabitants of the fortlet may well have kept it clean and clear of rubbish, dumping it elsewhere, and certainly it seems that midden waste was used in part to fill and level ditches at the end of Phase 1. This might represent the clearance of middens accumulated during the lifetime of the Phase 2 fortlet, although it has to be admitted that there is a significant lack of bone or other food waste within these fills.

The size of the Phase 2 fortlet makes clear the fact that it was not intended to house a large garrison, and thus that it probably played little part in the policing or organisation of the locality. To this end it must have always been something of an outpost, introverted, serving a specific function. The large structure within, although not extensively investigated, bears a resemblance to the towers encountered within a number of other fortlets and/or signal stations (eg Burgh-by-Sands, Daniels 1989), suggesting a similar purpose. Its proximity to the

70

estuary (perhaps as little as a 20 minute walk) might well suggest that the fortlet also served as lighthouse or beacon, marking the landfall.

It has been noted on numerous occasions that small ships require little in the way of permanent harbour facilities and can be beached with ease, especially in sheltered water where the tidal range is relatively great. Indeed, elsewhere ship-building was undertaken on the foreshore as late as the end of the nineteenth century (Falconer 1993, 73, with regard to the River Clyde; see Grape 1995, 94-96, 127-8 for an early medieval instance), requiring little in the way of permanent structures. Thus the lack of physical evidence for a harbour below Kirkham need not prove an impediment to any link between the fort and shipping.

Phase 3 appears to reflect a major change of scale (and function?) at Kirkham, when the fortlet was replaced by a much larger and more standard fort in the early second century. Almost all of the fort's interior lay outside the development area, as the encircling ramparts coincided for the most part with a modern land boundary. The ramparts were substantial and had probably survived as a significant barrier long enough to influence the development of later land divisions. They were built from stacked turf, revetted to the front with a sandstone facing, and probably to the back by cobbled walling, although it is equally possible that internal buildings backed directly onto the rampart. Modern housing on the site makes it unlikely that the interior will ever be extensively investigated.

Interestingly the Phase 2 fortlet appears to have been partly incorporated into the new structure, suggesting a continued use, although one of the large postholes associated with the interior structures was clearly sealed by the new earthen rampart, indicating at least a partial change in lay-out. Presumably this implies that Kirkham still looked to the sea and coastal communication.

The erection of the stone fort would have required an increased military work-force, presumably accommodated close by. Equally it must have necessitated the accumulation of large amounts of building materials, especially building stone, over a relatively short period. Red sandstone does not outcrop at Kirkham and would have had to be imported to the site, presumably representing considerable effort bringing the stone from Preston or Blackpool, where it outcrops today at sea-level (C Wells, pers comm); it is tempting to see it brought downriver to the site as ballast in ships or barges returning from Ribchester and Walton-le-Dale, or going up-river from Blackpool. It is not, however, impossible that it was brought by land along the road from Preston, or inland from Blackpool, raising interesting speculation on the origins and existence of the Dane's Pad.

Although little of the area within the fort could be excavated, it was clear that the surviving remains, fragmentary cobbled surfaces and ephemeral wall-lines, lay very close to the present ground surface and had undoubtedly been badly disturbed, presumably by stone robbing and agriculture. The fort lay within the town fields and it is not difficult to envisage it regarded as a common quarry.

The rampart was fronted by a single substantial ditch, apparently supplemented with outworks. Both the defensive ditch and the outworks were re-cut on two occasions, each time overlapping the preceding ditch and thereby suggesting that it was largely filled when re-cut. No environmental evidence was available from the fills of the earliest ditch, but the primary fill of the first re-cut probably reflects the local environment, heathland and grassland, and more specifically turf. There were, however, also numerous seeds of *Juncus squarrosus*, a rush confined to wet heaths and bogs and unknown in the vicinity today, suggesting that some element of the ditch fill was imported from elsewhere. The presence within the insect fauna of stag beetle, which now has a much more southerly distribution, suggests that the temperature may well have been consistently higher than it is today.

Later fills indicate that as the ditch filled it became more and more waterlogged, and even contained stretches of standing water, in which a great deal of material from the vicinity was allowed to accumulate, including ash, dung and stable manure and small fragments from a range of woody plants, alder, birch, oak, hazel and holly, presumably representing the composition of the local woodland under-growth. It is also very clear that a diverse mixture of material found its way into the later fills of this ditch, and further samples from the material suggestive of standing water indicated stable manure, open turf and a small amount of food waste (fig pips). Such a wide range must surely suggest that, in its later days, the first re-cut ditch was used as a convenient dumping place for an assortment of rubbish. A large dump of wood, incorporating a small amount of brushwood (hazel, oak, and willow), 40 or more tent pegs, and a *pilum muralis*, was also found within this waterlogged fill, which presumably suggests either that the ditch was regarded as a suitable repository for even relatively large objects, or that it was too unpleasant and treacherous to allow lost objects to be retrieved.

Both the defensive ditch and the outworks were re-cut for a second time late in the life of the fort and it is clear that the last fills of these ditches represent its decay, presumably some time after it had been abandoned, as antiquarians record that parts of the walls stood until relatively recent times (*see* account in Singleton 1980), perhaps suggesting that large-scale robbing was a late phenomenon. The later fills seem to have accumulated naturally with layers of silt slowly building up over tumbled stone from the collapsed masonry revetment.

The small amount of stone tumble remaining in the upper ditch fills suggests that the revetment must have been severely robbed, not surprising in an area short of good building stone, and the odd fragments of medieval pottery, for example, lying on a cobbled surface within the fort, rather imply that some of medieval Kirkham might have been built with stone from the fort.

A series of ditches to the east of the fort has been interpreted as evidence for an annexe. The fact that these follow a very similar sequence of refurbishment to those of the rampart ditch and the outworks presumably links them very closely to the fort, the whole complex perhaps re-dug each time. Environmental evidence from the primary fills again suggests that the area was covered with short acid grassland including heathgrass and *Potentilla* sp. Some of this might have derived from turves dumped into the ditch but it seems likely that turves, even if destined for building, would not have been brought from far afield. Perhaps their presence in the primary fills of the first annexe ditch might suggest that they were superfluous material from the construction of the earthen ramparts and, by extension, that this ditch was dug early on, perhaps to enclose an area within which the builders might have been accommodated or building materials stored, a possibility which has been explored with regard to the period of rebuilding in stone at Ribchester (Buxton and Howard-Davis forthcoming). It seems that the annexe remained in use throughout the relatively short lifetime of the stone fort (probably not much more than 40 years) although there is little to suggest to what use it was put.

Apart from this annexe, little coherent could be extracted from the somewhat jumbled archaeological sequences investigated outside the fort walls. The nature of extramural settlement has been much under investigation in recent years, mainly as a mechanism to explore the often unclear relationship between the inhabitants of the fort and civilians in the locality. Until recently it was accepted that a civilian settlement grew up almost organically around Roman forts as opportunist adventurers and entrepreneurs, and camp followers, created a shanty settlement under the protective eye of the fort, effectively there only to serve and service the troops. Such a view is now frequently challenged (for example Millet 1984), with the suggestion that in the early days of the Roman period in the North West, extramural settlement was carefully controlled and monitored by the fort (Olivier 1987, Newman *et al* forthcoming), almost to the extent of plantation settlements, accommodating not an influx of locals attracted to the delights of the Roman way of life, but civilians from elsewhere with particular talents required by the military establishment, almost 'lay' soldiers.

Evidence at Kirkham suggests that quite large parts of the immediate surrounds of the fort were cobbled, including the backfilled ditches of Phase 1, creating an effective *cordon sanitaire* around the fort (seen also at Ribchester) keeping civilian activity at a distance as well as providing a theatre for military show, parades, manoeuvres, and a marketplace (Jones 1984). Undoubtedly the cobbles also served to keep the fort environs relatively clean, cutting down on mud and the like in a very wet locality.

Kirkham was linked by a road running along the north bank of the river to the other forts of the Ribble Valley and there was likely to have been frequent contact. Indeed a comparison between second-century activity at Ribchester and at Kirkham suggests that their fates were closely linked, probably by some form of regulated trade which, it is tempting to suggest, might have been associated with whatever was produced at the industrial site at Walton-le-Dale (Gibbons and Howard-Davis forthcoming). Thus, the strong suggestion of heavy and systematic road traffic between the three Ribble Valley sites at Kirkham, Walton-le-Dale and Ribchester might well have necessitated extensive hard-standing around the fort. Other evidence of extramural activity is extremely nebulous, a hint of industrial activity in the form of a sunken hearth and work area, insubstantial walls and ditched enclosures, which make little sense in isolation.

Day-to-Day Life

The unusually sparse nature of the finds for a Roman site has allowed little speculation on the more intimate details of life at Kirkham and the amount of residuality caused by the repeated re-cutting and re-aligning of features made it impossible to detect any but the grossest chronological trends within either the pottery or the other finds.

A few points can, however, be made. Although some window glass, roof tile and hypocaust tile was found, suggesting one or more fairly sophisticated 'Romanised' buildings on or near the site, there were remarkably few iron nails, a mere ten, compared with thousands recovered from excavations at other Roman sites, like Ribchester (Buxton and Howard-Davis forthcoming), Lancaster (Newman *et al* forthcoming) or Papcastle (Quartermaine *et al* forthcoming). This lack, especially of the smallish all-purpose nails that were used extensively in carpentry and building, might imply a different building technique, for instance wattle and daub or the clay and cobble walling known from later buildings in the Fylde (Watson and McClintock 1979, 15). It still seems likely that some nails would have been used for doors and window frames etc, and perhaps the lack can be attributed to routine and extensive re-cycling of timber and nails, although this is not thought to have been particularly frequent on Roman sites as nails require re-forging, a process that negates the small saving on materials unless iron was in very short supply. It might signal the systematic dismantling of the fort when it was abandoned in the mid-second century (the vast hoard of nails at Inchtuthil (Manning 1985) appears to have been accumulated in this way) or it might signal extensive scavenging at a relatively early stage in the decay of the fort and extramural buildings.

The cache of tent pegs is a clear indication of less substantial structures, temporary accommodation for troops on the move or during periods of refurbishment.

Small amounts of fired clay and industrial residues were consistently encountered within features and fills of every phase, again suggesting, although sketchily, the presence of high temperature processes on the site; whether, however, they were truly industrial or routine, demand-led servicing cannot be ascertained. The industrial waste suggests secondary iron-working, probably routine blacksmithing of the kind which must have been undertaken at every fort and farmstead and required very little specialist provision beyond a small hearth and a bag of tools.

Very few glass vessels were noted, mainly the well-known small and sturdy blue-green mould-blown storage vessels which remained in use over an extended period between the first and third centuries AD, although one fragment suggests the use of some finer tableware, specifically a colourless cylindrical cup in vogue from the mid-second century onwards. Whilst a slightly greater range of glass tablewares might have been expected, especially during the early period when a reasonable range of fine ceramic tablewares including decorated samian were present in the pottery assemblage, glass appears to have been routinely re-cycled during the Roman period, and the lack might simply reflect an efficient recycling system.

Fine metalwork was almost absent, only two very badly damaged brooches were found; the lack of military equipment is marked, although under normal circumstances this does not appear in great quantities on any site since soldiers looked after their equipment and were unlikely to lose or discard their kit. The lack of general metalwork, however, might reflect low status with little of value there to be lost. The same might be argued for the lack of coins; perhaps the local inhabitants were poor enough to search exhaustively even for lost coins of the lowest denomination. Indeed, if much of the site was simply grazed by local farmers, the use of Roman coinage need not have been favoured or necessary in daily life, especially for those at the lower end of the social scale such as herdsmen.

The pottery in use at the site during all phases appears entirely typical of the range found at most Roman military sites in the North West and elsewhere during the late first and second centuries. A great deal of it was imported, showing a reliance on suppliers to the south and in Gaul. As has been noted, a very small amount of hand-made pottery, undoubtedly a local native product, was found in an early ditch fill in a context that makes it possible to suggest that it was not used specifically at the fort. Otherwise cooking vessels and tablewares all derive from the usual range of early producers, the closest probably Wilderspool, which, it is thought, did not come on-stream until the last first to early second century.

There is an interesting difference between the date range of the coarsewares and that of the samian ware, which suggests a significantly earlier start date for occupation of the site. Although much of the earlier samian pottery derives from the two major South Gaulish production centres at La Graufesenque and Montans, it is interesting to see relatively large amounts from early (pre-export period) production at the Central Gaulish sites of Lezoux and Les Martres-de-Veyre (*see* Chapter 7: Samian). The presence of such vessels on British sites is usually accounted for as representing the loss of personal possessions bought in Gaul and brought over by individuals. The amount at Kirkham, however (three vessels), begins to belie this suggestion and its presence at a putative landing point at an early date might suggest that the occasional load was exported from Lezoux, possibly hawked from port to port in mixed cargoes rather than as part of the large contract cargoes which seem to characterise the Pottery's later commercial dealings (Greene 1986, 167).

The consistent 'Roman' make-up of pottery assemblages might suggest a cultural conservatism amongst the troops that must surely have largely isolated and cushioned them from their surrounds, providing a consistent and attainable way of life wherever they were stationed, and indeed the vast military contracts that brought diagnostically Roman vessels such as mortaria and products like Black Burnished ware to sites like Kirkham may have been intended to service such a desire for constancy amongst its troops, incidentally reinforcing a 'Roman' identity, even for auxiliary troops, and, by extension, reinforcing their 'differentness' from local native groups. Such a cultural security blanket tends to mask the origins of various garrisons extremely effectively and so, without supplementary evidence, there is little to suggest who was stationed at the fort.

The same set of cultural expectations presumably held good with regard to foodstuffs and local produce seems only ever to have supplemented the more standard grain (often transported in bulk over surprisingly long distances) and beef diet. Although literary evidence from Vindolanda (largely contemporary with Kirkham) suggests a wide and attractive diet (Bowman 1994, Bowman and Thomas 1994, *Vindol Tab II*. 191, *II*. 302), it is noticeable that considerable effort was made to import certain Mediterranean products, especially olives and olive oil, fish sauce and wine, in very large quantities. These products, or at least the distinctive amphorae in which they were transported and stored, appear even at out-of-the-way sites in the furthest reaches of the empire. Figs, too, seem to have been sought by the soldiery, though whether as a pleasant sweetmeat or as a medicinal laxative is not clear.

Very little animal bone has survived on the site, a not-uncommon phenomenon in the soils of north-west England. Heavily calcined (burnt) bone has a far greater tendency to survive than unburnt, suggesting that the assemblage is more likely to represent food waste disposed of by burning than the full range of fauna present on the site. Most of the burnt bone derived from Phase 1 contexts and thus can only reflect an element of the diet at that time. Cattle and sheep/goat were identified, although in quantities too small to allow further conclusions. Environmental evidence strongly suggests the presence of horses, although none were identified within the bone assemblage; depositional circumstance may well have created this lack as there seems to have been a strong Roman cultural preference against the consumption of horse meat (Dannell and Wild 1987), much reducing the likelihood of burnt horse bone.

Interestingly, the remains of two dogs were noted (from Phase 3 contexts); in neither case was the bone burnt. One was represented by a single bone, bearing what might have been a deliberate cut-mark, whilst the other was a substantial part of the skeleton of a small, bow-legged, terrier-type dog of the kind that might have been kept for hunting, ratting and the like. Despite the cut-mark, it is unlikely that either animal was consumed as food, but one may perhaps have been skinned; dog-skin is on occasion tanned and used for clothing, and is still today favoured in some places for drum heads (eg the Irish *bodhran*).

The Place of Kirkham within the Region

It seems possible to suggest that the first temporary camp may have been erected during, or in the wake of, the Agricolan advance as troops arrived by sea to supplement the northern campaigns. There may then have been brief periods of abandonment, but it is likely that the small fortlet-cum-signal station was built soon after, serving to mark and patrol safe landfall beneath the site, to the south, in the Ribble estuary. On occasion, the arrival by sea of new troops would have necessitated the renewal or re-building of temporary accommodation, which in between appears to have become overgrown, used not only by the garrison, but probably also by locals, as convenient grazing.

This provision appears to have been sufficient until the early second century (around AD 120) when a new and much larger stone fort was erected on the same site as the fortlet. The fact that the fort required both outworks and a defended annexe might suggest that it was expected to undertake more contentious activities than hitherto. The incorporation of the original fortlet within the new fort might also suggest that the original function of the fortlet (possibly a lighthouse) retained its importance. The rationale behind this enlargement is unclear, but may well have been linked to increased road and river commerce with other Roman sites in the Ribble Valley and sea ports within a day's sail to the north and south. What is, however, clear, is that the change was short-lived, and the fort went out of use, either dismantled or abandoned to decay, by the mid-second century, a lifetime of little more than 30 years.

Little coherent evidence could be gathered for the extramural activity associated with the fort, beyond an assertion of its existence. It seems, however, that the short life of the fort was inadequate to impart to it sufficient impetus to survive as an independent settlement, although it is more than likely that it outlived the fort, fading away in the later second or early third century.

Thus far the fort at Kirkham has been viewed largely in isolation. It has become clear, however, that its existence relied on interaction with its neighbours and presumably with farther flung places in the Roman communication and trade networks, rather than on any innate strategic importance of its location.

In recent years it has become more and more obvious that the conventional view of the Agricolan invasion of north-western England is to an extent an historical construct, based on a too convenient acceptance of the accounts of Tacitus. Excavations at Ribchester, Lancaster and Carlisle have all now established pre-Agricolan activity, often at an apparently fairly wealthy level, apparently intending to impress. This suggests strongly that the Roman presence in the tribal area of Brigantia was relatively widespread, probably as much an exercise in Public Relations as anything else. Indeed, it now seems possible that Agricola was treading a well-established path as he completed the annexation of the North in the late AD 70s.

Evidence shows that Ribchester, whose later fortune appears to have been closely allied to that of Kirkham, was founded in the early AD 70s (Buxton and Howard-Davis forthcoming). There is no doubt as to its strategic significance, not only guarding a ford on the Ribble, but straddling a major cross-roads (Margary 1957) of routes that almost without doubt existed long before they were formalised by the Romans. It policed the main north-south route along the western flank of the Pennines, as well as a principal route eastwards across the Pennines to York and Aldborough. The latter road also continued west from Ribchester to Kirkham, and was presumably built solely to link the two forts. Attempts to extend the line of the road significantly beyond Kirkham, however, to the Fylde coast or the mouth of the River Wyre, have proved inconclusive (Middleton et al 1995).

Various suggestions have been made to account for the location of a fort at Kirkham, which appears somewhat adrift from the general arrangement of forts in the region, which are generally orientated upon arterial roads. It has been argued that it was not intended to guard the lowest ford of the Ribble, as prevailing conditions at the time would have rendered the ford strategically valueless if not non-existent. The Fylde has never been an area of particular wealth, either from natural resources or agriculture, and it can perhaps be assumed that, if the Romans particularly valued the wetland resource for some reason, a fort might well have been built to the south as well, amidst the vast wetlands of West Lancashire. The only obvious reason for a fort at Kirkham would be as a potential entreport, at the mouth of a substantial river, navigable to large ships at least as far as Preston and presumably further upriver by barge or road. Thus Kirkham might have provided an invaluable staging point, allowing sea-borne goods relatively rapid and easy access to the road system via Ribchester.

Tacitus makes specific mention of estuaries in his account of Agricola's advance (Agricola 20, 2); this might be taken to suggest that they were regarded as of special importance or relevance to his progress, but might equally reflect a stereotypical account of difficult terrain. The possibility that Agricola in fact used land and sea forces *in tandem* during the advance, landing troops at convenient points and marching them inland, has already been raised (Shotter 1994) and it has been argued that Kirkham owes its existence to that strategy. Further, it seems likely that, rather than sail his troops into *terra incognita*, Agricola would have based his judgement and choice of disembarkation point in part on his own knowledge of the area, and in part on that of coastal traders already using the long-established seaways of the Irish Sea Province. It is of interest that the safe harbourages marked by Roman forts at Chester on the Dee, Kirkham on the Ribble, Lancaster on the Lune (Watercrook on the Kent and Ravenglass on the Esk, Irt and Mite, although these are both appreciably later), and ultimately Carlisle on the Solway, are all around a day's sailing apart and all provide access inland in otherwise difficult country. Similarly, a detour around the Wirral, from Dee to Mersey, would link Wilderspool into the same chain of sites. It is interesting to speculate as to whether we can thus begin to reconstruct the sea trading routes of the north-west coast.

Mills (Chapter 7) has suggested a link between second century Montans ware (found at Kirkham) and the importation of late South Gaulish samian through a western port; the same arguments presumably apply for the import of early Central Gaulish products, suggesting an established route around the west coast for pottery from Gaul, either in bulk or as parts of mixed cargoes. Gaulish coarsewares would, presumably, have taken the same route and even travelled in the same cargoes.

There is also a likelihood of heavy commercial traffic between Ribchester and Kirkham in the early years of the second century, about the time that the signal station/fortlet at Kirkham was much expanded and the fort at Ribchester re-built, and it is worthy of note that, when that connection waned or was broken, Kirkham was abandoned and Ribchester fell into a decline and its extramural settlement appears to have changed focus, turning away from the Kirkham road. Whilst the trade cannot be characterised, it is tempting to link it in some way with the industrial site at Walton-le-Dale, where activity peaked in the second century (Gibbons and Howard-Davis forthcoming). Whilst it is difficult to define what was produced at Walton-le-Dale, if one regards Wilderspool to the south as at least a rough comparator, then a range of goods, day-to-day necessities such as pottery and glass, were obviously produced in bulk for export (Hinchcliffe and Williams 1989).

It is unlikely that it will ever be possible to establish why the fort at Kirkham was abandoned. What is clear is that the latter part of the second century was, in the North West, a period of covert unrest, possibly hinted at by the nebulous second Brigantian revolt around AD 150 (Wacher 1974, 50; Breeze and Dobson 1985), although this event is frequently called into question by numerous scholars. The rise of Carlisle as *civitas* capital successor to Aldborough in Yorkshire in the third century may well have been an indirect result of such turbulence, which is likely to have have involved considerable administrative reorganisation. It may be that east-west trade and commerce declined as a result of the change, reducing the need for a fort with little other strategic significance, and where the potential for a thriving civilian settlement appears not to have been realised; thus Kirkham may simply have been rationalised out of existence, and its sea-borne trade relocated further north to Lancaster, which thrived as a port well into the fourth century, and possibly even later (Jones and Shotter 1988).

The excavations at Kirkham have amply justified themselves. They were undertaken during a very restricted period, in advance of development, in an area about which little was known. Despite this they have achieved not only their original broad academic aims, but have allowed the unpublished earlier excavations of a local society to be further interpreted, linking in neatly to create an outline description of the stone fort. Further, in the present climate of academic re-assessment, they have allowed informed speculation on a number of points, not least coastal trade in the early Roman period and the relationship between Kirkham and its near neighbours. Until recently such speculation would not have been possible, as the range of information provided today by even small modern professional excavations and a synthetic approach to the interpretation of all strands of information simply did not exist (Reece 1995). Kirkham has demonstrated emphatically that even small, developer-funded investigations can add significantly to academic debate and the attempt to reconstruct and understand the first years of the Roman occupation and settlement of the North West.

BIBLIOGRAPHY

Allison, EP, Hutchinson, A, Jones, AKG, Kenward, HK, and Morgan, LM, 1991 in MR McCarthy, *Roman waterlogged remains at Castle street, Carlisle*, Cumberland Westmorland Antiq Archaeol Soc, Res Ser, **5**, Main text and Fascicle 1, Kendal

Allison, EP, and Kenward, HK, in press The insect remains, in (ed) I Caruana, *Excavations at Annetwell Street, Carlisle*

Anderson, AC, 1980 *A guide to Roman fine wares*, Leicester

Atkinson, D, 1914 A hoard of Samian ware from Pompeii, *J Roman Stud,* **4**, 27-64

Austen, PS, 1994 Recent excavations on Hadrian's Wall at Burgh-by-Sands, *Trans Cumberland Westmorland Antiq Archaeol Soc* n ser, **94**, 35-59

Baatz, D, 1975 *Der Römische Limes*, Berlin

Balfour-Browne, F, 1958 *British water beetles,* **3**, London

Bennett, J, 1982 The Great Chesters 'pilum murale', *Archaeol Aeliana* 5 ser, **10**, 200-204

Bishop, MC, and Coulston, JCN, 1993 *Roman military equipment*, London

Booth, RG, 1981 A second British colony of *Helophorus tuberculatus* Gyll, (Col., Hydrophilidae), *Entomologist's Monthly Mag,* **117**, 26

Bowman, AK, 1994 *Life and letters on the Roman frontier*, London

Bowman, AK and Thomas, JD, 1994 *Tabulae Vindolandenses II*, London

Breeze, D, and Dobson, B, 1985 Roman military deployment in Northern England, *Britannia,* **16**, 1-21

Buxton, KM, 1994 *Dowbridge Close Kirkham Lancashire: post-excavation assessment*, unpubl rep

Buxton, KM, and Howard-Davis, CLE, 1994 A *'pilum muralis'* from Kirkham, Lancashire, *ARMA,* **6.1**, 9-10

Buxton, KM, and Howard-Davis, CLE, forthcoming *Ribchester: excavations in 1980 and 1989-90*, Lancaster Imprints

Casey, PJ, 1992 The monetization of a third world economy: money supply in Britain in the first century AD, in (eds) M Wood and F Queiroza, *Current research on the Romanization of the Western Provinces*, BAR Int Ser, **575**, 95-101, Oxford

Clark, JT, 1967 The distribution of *Lucanus cervus* (L.) (Col., Lucanidae) in Britain, *Entomologist's Monthly Mag,* **102** (for 1966), 199-204

Coles, BJ, and Coles, JM, 1989 *People of the Wetlands: Bogs, Bodies and Lake Dwellers*, London

Collingwood, RG, and Richmond, I, 1976 *The Archaeology of Roman Britain*, rev edn, London

Collingwood, RG, and Taylor, MV, 1928 Roman Britain in 1928, *J Roman Stud*, **18**, 191-214

Croston, J (ed), 1893 *The history of the County Palatine and Duchy of Lancaster*, by E Baines, rev edn, London

Dainton, M, 1992 A quick, semi-quantitative method for recording nematode gut parasite eggs from archaeological deposits, *Circaea, Bull Ass Envir Archaeol*, **9**, 58-63

Daniels, C, 1989 *The eleventh pilgrimage of Hadrian's Wall*, Newcastle upon Tyne

Dannell, GB, and Wild, JP, 1987 *Longthorpe II. The military works depot: an episode in landscape history*, Britannia Monog, **8**, London

Dickinson, B, 1990 The samian ware, in MR McCarthy, *A Roman, Anglian and Medieval Site at Blackfriars Street*, Cumberland Westmorland Antiq Archaeol Soc, Res Ser, **4**, 213-236, Kendal

Dickinson, B, The samian, in KM Buxton and CLE Howard-Davis forthcoming

Dixon, A, 1949 *Portus Setantiorum*, unpubl doc, Fleetwood Lib

Dixon, KR, and Southern, P, 1992 *The Roman cavalry*, London

Edwards, BJN, Webster, PV, Jones, GDB, and Wild, JP, 1985 Excavation on the western defences and in the interior, 1970, in (eds) BJN Edwards and PV Webster, *Ribchester excavations part 1 – Excavations within the Roman fort 1970-80*, 19-40, Cardiff

Falconer, J, 1993 *Sail and Steam. A century of sea-faring enterprise 1840-1935*, London

Farrer, W, and Brownbill, J, 1912 *The Victoria History of the County of Lancaster*, **7**, London

Faull, ML, and Stinson, M (eds), 1986 Yorkshire, in (ed) J Morris, *Domesday Book*, **30**, 2 vols, Chichester

Fisher, RA, Corbet, AS, and Williams, CB, 1943 The relation between the number of species and the number of individuals in a random sample of an animal population, *J Animal Ecol*, **12**, 42-58

Gibbons, P, and Howard-Davis, CLE, forthcoming, *Excavations at Walton-le-Dale*

Gillam, JP, 1970 *Types of coarse pottery vessels in Northern Britain*, Newcastle upon Tyne

Gillam, JP, 1976 Coarse fumed ware in Northern Britain, *Glasgow Archaeol J*, **4**, 57-80

Gilliver, CM, 1993 Hedgehogs, calthrops and palisade stakes, *J Roman Military Stud*, **4**, 49-54

Goodwin, K, Huntley, JP, Allison, EP, Kenward, HK, and Morgan, LM, 1991 The plant and insect remains from Building 1090, in MR McCarthy, *Roman waterlogged remains at Castle street, Carlisle*, Cumberland Westmorland Antiq Archaeol Soc, Res Ser, **5**, Fascicle 1, 22-4 , Kendal

Grape, W, 1995 *The Bayeux Tapestry. Monument to a Norman Triumph*, London

Green, M, 1992 *Animals in Celtic life and myth*, London

Greene, K, 1986 *The archaeology of the Roman economy*, London

Hall, AR, and Kenward, HK, 1990 Environmental evidence from the Colonia: General Accident and Rougier Street, *The Archaeology of York*, CBA Res Rep, **14**(6), London

Hall, DG, 1970 *Lucanus cervus* (L.) (Col., Lucanidae) in Britain, *Entomologist's Monthly Mag*, **105**, 183-4

Hansen, M, 1987 The Hydrophiloidea (Coleoptera) of Fennoscandia and Denmark, *Fauna Entomologica Scandinavica*, **18**, Leiden and Copenhagen

Hattatt, R, 1985, *Iron Age and Roman brooches*, Oxford

Harcourt, RA, 1974 The dog in prehistoric and early historic Britain, *J Archaeol Sci*, **1**, 151-175

Harland, J (ed), 1868-1870 *The History of the County Palatine and Duchy of Lancaster*, by E Baines, rev edn, London

Hartley, KF, and Webster, PV, 1973 Romano-British pottery kilns near Wilderspool, *Archaeol J*, **13**, 77-103

Haselgrove, CC, 1996 The Iron Age, in (ed) R Newman, *The Archaeology of Lancashire*, 61-74, Lancaster

Hermet, F, 1934 *La Graufesenque (Condatomago)*, Paris

Higham, N, 1986 *The northern counties to AD 1000*, London

Hinchcliffe, J, and Williams, JH, 1989 *Roman Warrington*, Brigantia Monog, **2**, Manchester

Hinde, T (ed), 1986 *The Domesday Book. England's heritage, then and now*, London

Hird, L, forthcoming a, The Roman pottery, in KM Buxton and CLE Howard-Davis forthcoming

Hird, L, forthcoming b, The Roman pottery, in P Gibbons and CLE Howard-Davis forthcoming

Hodgkinson, DF, 1993 *Dowbridge Close, Kirkham, Lancashire, archaeological evaluation*, unpubl rep

Howard-Davis, CLE, forthcoming The wood, in KM Buxton and CLE Howard-Davis forthcoming

Isings, C, 1957 *Roman glass from dated finds*, Groningen

Jessop, L, 1986 *Dung beetles and chafers. Coleoptera: Scarabaeoidea*, Handbooks for the identification of British insects, **5**(11), London

Johns, C, 1993 Samian, in WH Manning, *Report on the excavations at Usk. The Roman Pottery*, Cardiff

Jones, GDB, 1984 Becoming different without knowing it. The role and development of *vici*, in (eds) TFC Blagg and AC King, *Military and Civilian in Roman Britain*, BAR Brit, **136**, 75-92, Oxford

Jones, GDB, and Shotter, DCA, 1988 *Roman Lancaster: rescue archaeology in an historic city 1970-75*, Brigantia Monog, **1**, Manchester

Kenward, HK, 1976 *Helophorus tuberculatus* Gyll. (Col., Hydrophilidae) in the City of York, *Entomologist's Monthly Mag*, **111**, 92

Kenward, HK, 1984 *Helophorus tuberculatus* Gyll. (Col., Hydrophilidae) from Roman Carlisle, *Entomologist's Monthly Mag*, **120**, 225

Kenward, HK, 1988 *Helophorus tuberculatus* Gyll. (Col., Hydrophilidae) from Roman York, *Entomologist's Monthly Mag*, **124**, 90

Kenward, HK, 1992 Rapid recording of archaeological insect remains - a reconsideration, *Circaea, Bull Ass Envir Archaeol*, **9**, 81-8

Kenward, HK, and Allison, E, 1995 *Insect remains from the Roman fort at Papcastle, Cumbria*, AML Rep **95/1**, unpubl rep

Kenward, HK, Allison, EP, Dainton, M, Kemenes, IK, and Carrott, JB, 1992 *Evidence from insect remains and parasite eggs from Old Grapes Lane A, The Lanes, Carlisle*, AML Rep **78/92**, unpubl rep

Kenward, HK, Allison, EP, Morgan, LM, Jones, AKG, and Hutchinson, AR, 1991 The insect and parasite remains, in MR McCarthy, *Roman waterlogged remains at Castle street, Carlisle*, Cumberland Westmorland Antiq Archaeol Soc, Res Ser, **5**, Fascicle 1, 65-72, Kendal

Kenward, HK, Dainton, M, Kemenes, IK, and Carrott, JB, 1992a *Evidence from insect remains and parasite eggs from the Old Grapes Lane B site, The Lanes, Carlisle*, AML Rep **76/92**, unpubl rep

Kenward, HK, Dainton, M, Kemenes, IK, and Carrott, JB, 1992b *Evidence from insect remains and parasite eggs from the Lewthwaites Lane A site, The Lanes, Carlisle*, AML Rep **77/92**, unpubl rep

Kenward, HK, Engleman, C, Robertson, A, and Large, F, 1986 Rapid scanning of urban archaeological deposits for insect remains, *Circaea, Bull Ass Envir Archaeol*, **3**, 163-72

Kenward, HK, Hall, AR, and Jones, AKG, 1980 A tested set of techniques for the extraction of plant and animal macrofossils from waterlogged archaeological deposits, *Sci Archaeol*, **22**, 3-15

Kloet, GS, and Hincks, WD, 1964-77 *A check list of British insects*, 2nd edn, London

Knorr, R, 1919 *Töpfer und Fabriken verzierter Terra-Sigillata des ersten Jahrhunderts*, Stuttgart

Knorr, R, 1952 *Terra-sigillata-Gefässe des ersten Jahrhunderts mit Töpfernamen*, Stuttgart

Large, F, Kenward, HK, Carrott, J, Nicholson, C, and Kent, P, 1994 *Insect and other invertebrate remains from the Roman fort at Ribchester, Lancashire (site code RB89)*, Environmental Archaeology Unit, York **94/11**, unpubl rep

McCarthy, MR, 1993 *Carlisle: History and Guide*, Gloucester

Manning, WH, 1985 The iron objects, in LF Pitts and JK St Joseph, *Inchtuthil. The Roman legionary fortress*, Britannia Monog, **6**, 289-99, London

Manning, WH, 1986 *Catalogue of the Romano-British Iron Tools, Fittings and Weapons in the British Museum*, London

Margary, ID, 1957 *Roman Roads in Britain. Vol II. North of the Foss Way - Bristol Channel (inc Wales and Scotland)*, London

Marsh, G, 1981 London's samian supply and its relationship to the development of the Gallic samian industry, in (eds) AC Anderson and AS Anderson, *Roman pottery research in Britain and North-west Europe*, BAR Int Ser, **123**(i), 173-238, Oxford

Mattingly, H, Sydenham, EA, and Sutherland, CHV (eds), 1923-84 *The Roman imperial coinage*, London

Middleton, R (ed), 1990, *North West Wetlands Survey Annual Report 1990*, Lancaster

Middleton, R, 1992, Excavations on the line of Kate's Pad at Brook Farm Pilling, 1991, in E Huckerby, C Wells, and R Middleton, Recent Palaeoecological and archaeological work in Over Wyre, Lancashire, in R Middleton (ed), *North West Wetlands Survey Annual Report, 1992*, 9-11, Lancaster

Middleton, R, and Tooley, MJ, forthcoming *The Wetlands of South West Lancashire*, Lancaster Imprints

Middleton, R, Wells, C, and Huckerby, E, 1995 *The wetlands of North Lancashire*, Lancaster Imprints, **4**, Lancaster

Millet, M, 1984 Forts and the origins of towns: cause or effect? in (eds) TFC Blagg and AC King, *Military and Civilian in Roman Britain*, BAR Brit Ser, **136**, 65-74, Oxford

Milne, G, 1982 Recording timberwork on the London waterfront, in (ed) S McGrail, *Woodworking techniques before 1500 AD*, BAR Int Ser, **129**, 7-24, Oxford

Newman, RM, Hair, N, Howard-Davis, CLE, and Miller, I, forthcoming *Excavations at Mitchell's Brewery, Lancaster*

Olivier, ACH, 1987 Postscript: the nature of the Ribchester civil settlement, in (eds) BJN Edwards and PV Webster, *Ribchester excavations part II. Excavations in the civil settlement. A. The structures*, 117-126, Cardiff

Oswald, F, 1936-7 *Index of figure-types on Terra Sigillata (Samian ware)*, Liverpool

Peacock, DPS, and Williams, DF, 1986 *Amphorae and the Roman economy*, London

Perring, FH, and Walters, SM, 1962 *Atlas of the British flora*, London

Planck, D, 1975 *Neue Ausgrabungen an Limes*, Stuttgart

Potter, TW, 1975 Excavations at Bowness on Solway, *Trans Cumberland Westmorland Antiq Archaeol Soc, n ser*, **75**, 29-57

Quartermaine, H, Howard-Davis, CLE, and Olivier, ACH, forthcoming *Excavations at Papcastle, 1984*

Reece, R, 1995 Bones, bangles and barbarians: towards the perfect cemetery report, *Antiquity,* **69,** 263

Rigby, V, 1973 Potters' stamps on Terra Nigra and Terra Rubra found in Britain, in (ed) A Detsicas, *Current research in Romano-British Pottery* CBA Res Rep, **10,** 7-24, London

Rogers, GR, 1974 *Poteries Sigillées de la Gaule Centrale I. Les motifs non figurées,* Gallia suppl, **28,** Paris

Shotter, DCA, 1984, *Roman North-west England,* Centre North West Reg Stud Occ Pap, **14,** Lancaster

Shotter, DCA, 1993 *Romans and Britons in North West England,* Lancaster

Shotter, DCA, 1994 Rome and the Brigantes: Early hostilities, *Trans Cumberland Westmorland Antiq Archaeol Soc, n ser,* **94,** 21-39

Shotter, DCA, 1995 *Roman Coins from North West England: First Supplement,* Lancaster

Shotter, DCA, 1997 *Romans and Britons in North West England,* rev edn, Lancaster

Singleton, FJ, 1980 *Kirkham. A short history,* Lytham St Annes

Sisson, S, and Grossman, JD, 1975 *Anatomy of the domestic animals,* London

Smith, AJE, 1978 *The moss flora of Britain and Ireland,* Cambridge

Stallibrass, S, forthcoming, Animal bone, in KM Buxton and CLE Howard-Davis forthcoming

Stanfield, JA, and Simpson, G, 1990 *Les potiers de la Gaule Centrale,* Paris

Sutherland, CHV, 1936 Three Roman Coin Hoards, *Num Chron,* 5 ser, **16,** 316-20

Tacitus, trans H Mattingley, 1948 *Tacitus on Britain and Germany,* London

Terrisse, JR, 1968 *Les céramique sigillées gallo-romaine des Martres-de-Veyre (Puy de Dôme),* Gallia suppl, **19,** Paris

Tooley, M, 1980 Theories of Coastal Change in North-West England, in (ed) FH Thompson, *Archaeology and Coastal Change,* Soc Antiq London Occ Pap, n ser, **1,** 74-86

Toynbee, JMC, 1962 *Art in Roman Britain,* London

Tutin, TG, Heywood, VH, Burgess, WA, Valentine, DH, Walters, SM, and Webb, DA, 1964-81 *Flora Europaea,* **1-5,** Cambridge

van Driel Murray, C, 1990 New light on old tents, *J Roman Military Equip Stud,* **1,** 109-138

Vegetius, trans NP Milner, 1993 *Epitome of Military Science,* Liverpool

Wacher, JS, 1974 *The towns of Roman Britain*, London

Watkin, WT, 1883 *Roman Lancashire*, Liverpool

Watson, RC, and McClintock, ME, 1979 *Traditional Houses of the Fylde*, Centre North West Reg Stud Occ Pap, **6**, Lancaster

Webster, G, 1979 *The Imperial Roman Army*, 2nd edn, London

Wells, C, Huckerby, E, and Hall, V, 1997 Mid- and late- Holocene vegetation, history and tephra studies at Fenton Cottage, Lancashire, UK, *Veg, Hist Archaeol Bot*, **6(13)**, 153-66

Whitaker, J, 1773 *The History of Manchester*, Manchester

Whitaker, TD, 1823 *History of Richmondshire...together with...the Wapentakes of Lonsdale, Ewecross and Amunderness*, Liverpool

Williams, DF, 1977 The Romano-British Black Burnished industry: an essay on characterization by Heavy Mineral Analysis, in (ed) DPS Peacock, *Pottery and early commerce: characterization and trade in Roman and later ceramics*, 163-220, London

Wilson, DG, 1988 Horse dung from Roman Lancaster, in Jones and Shotter 1988, 170-78

Wilson, DR, 1984, Defensive Outworks of Roman Forts in Britain, *Britannia,* **15**, 51-62

Woodward, PJ, Davies, SM, and Graham, AH, 1993 *Excavations at Greyhound Yard, Dorchester 1981-4*, Dorset Nat Hist Archaeol Soc Monog, **12**, Dorchester

APPENDIX 1
SUMMARY CONTEXT INDEX

In the following, the context number is followed by the Trench in which it was identified, then a brief description. Contexts in italics are identical to others. Context numbers not mentioned in the list were not used.

Natural subsoils

116:A:Layer:-:natural:clay
066:A:Same as 116
067:A:Same as 116
068:A:Same as 116
069:A:Same as 116
298:E:Same as 116
498:T:Same as 116
499:T:Same as 116

Phase 1.1

015:A:Pit:cut:-:-
016:A:Pit 015:fill:-:clay
017:A:Pit 015:fill:-:sandy loam
042:A:Hollow:cut:-:-
043:A:Hollow 042:fill:-:silty clay

060:A:Linear slot:cut:-:-
061:A:Linear slot 060:fill:-:clay

062:A:Linear feature:cut:-:-
063:A:Linear feature 062:fill:-:clay

064:A:Linear slot:cut:-:-
065:A: Linear slot 064:fill:-:silty clay

081:A:Linear slot:cut:-:-
082:A:Linear slot 081:fill:-:silty clay

083:A:Linear slot:cut:-:-
084:A:Linear slot 083:fill:-:silty clay

102:A:Linear slot:cut:-:-
103:A:Linear slot 102:fill:-:sandy clay

135:D:Hollow or ditch:cut:-:-
205:D:Same as 135
137:D:Hollow or ditch 135:fill:-:clay
196:D:Hollow or ditch 135:fill:-:silty clay
197:D:Hollow or ditch 135:fill:-:sandy clay
200:D:Hollow or ditch 135:fill:-:silty clay
201:D:Hollow or ditch 135:fill:-:silty clay
202:D:Hollow or ditch 135:fill:-:sandy silt
206:D:Hollow or ditch 135:fill:-:silty clay
208:D:Hollow or ditch 135:fill:-:cobbles
209:D:Hollow or ditch 135:fill:-:silty clay
256:D:Hollow or ditch 135:fill:-:silty clay
257:D:Hollow or ditch 135:fill:-:silty clay
258:D:Hollow or ditch 135:fill:-:silty clay
259:D:Same as 201

Phase 1:2

023:A:Palisade or revetment trench:cut:-:-
033:A: Same as 023
024:A:Palisade or revetment
034:A: Same as 024
023:fill:-:silty clay

032:A:Palisade or revetment 023:fill:-:cobble
039:A: Part of 023

037:A:Palisade or revetment trench:cut:-:-
038:A:Palisade or revetment 037:fill:-:silty clay

052:A:Ditch southern return:cut:-:-
195:D:Same as 052 (western return)
254:D:Same as 052 (western return)
053:A:Ditch 052 southern return:fill:-:silty clay
108:A:Ditch 052 southern return:fill:-:silty clay
109:A:Ditch 052 southern return:fill:-:silty clay
110:A:Ditch 052 southern return:fill:-:silty clay
111:A:Ditch 052 southern return:fill:-:silty clay
112:A:Ditch 052 southern return:fill:-:sandy silty clay
113:A:Ditch 052 southern return:fill:-:silty clay
114:A:Ditch 052 southern return:fill:-:silty clay
115:A:Ditch 052 southern return:fill:-:silty clay
136:D:Ditch 052 western return:fill:-:silty clay
255:D:Same as 136
198:D:Ditch 052 western return:fill:-:silty clay
199:D:Ditch 052 western return:fill:-:silty clay

012:A:Ditch 052 upcast:-:redeposited natural:clay

228:H:Ditch:cut:-:-
229:H:Ditch 228:fill:-:silty clay loam

302:H:Ditch:cut:-:-
347:H:Ditch 302:fill:-:sandy silty clay
348:H:Ditch 302:fill:-:silty clay-redeposited
349:H:Ditch 302:fill:-:silt

363:H:Hollow:cut:-:-
364:H:Hollow 363:fill:-:silty sand
365:H:Hollow 363:fill:-:silty clay

Phase 1:3

006:A:Ditch southern return:cut:-:-
013:A: Same as 006
308:K:Same as 006 (southern return)
224:E/H:Same as 006 (southern return)
336:L:Same as 006 (western return):cut:-:-
007:A:Ditch 006 southern return:fill:-:silty clay loam
014:A: Same as 007
059:A:Same as 007
058:A:Ditch 006 southern return fill:-:clay

090:A:Ditch 006 southern return:fill:-
:sandy silty clay
091:A:Ditch 006 southern return:fill:-
:sandy silty clay
098:A:Ditch 006 southern return:fill:-:silty
clay loam
099:A:Ditch 006 southern return:fill:-:silty
clay
100:A:Ditch 006 southern return:fill:-:silty
clay
101:A:Ditch 006 southern return:fill:-
:sandy clay loam
225:E/H:Ditch 006 southern return:fill:-
:sandy clay
226:E/H:Ditch 006 southern return:fill:-
:silty clay
227:E/H:Ditch 006 southern return:fill:-
:clay
230:E/H:Ditch 006 southern return:fill:-
:clay
281:E/H:Ditch 006 southern return:fill:-
:silty clay
282:E/H:Ditch 006 southern return:fill:-
:silty clay
283:E/H:Ditch 006 southern return:fill:-
:clay
313:K:Ditch 006 southern return:fill:-:silty
clay
314:K:Ditch 006 southern return:fill:-:clay
315:K:Ditch 006 southern return:fill:-:silty
clay
337:L:Ditch 006 western return:fill:-:sandy
clay
338:L:Ditch 006 western return:fill:-
:organic
339:L:Ditch 006 western return:fill:-:sand
342:L:Ditch 006 western return:fill:-:clay

129:A:Re-cut, ditch 006:cut:- :-
316:K:Same as 129
080:A:Re-cut 129:fill:-:silty clay
309:K:Re-cut 129:fill:-:silty clay and cobbles
310:K:Re-cut 129:fill:-:silty clay
311:K:Re-cut 129:fill:-:silty sandy clay
312:K:Re-cut 129:fill:-:silty clay

004:A:Ditch:cut:-:-
092:A: Same as 004
005:A:Ditch 004:fill:-:silty clay
093:A:Same as 005

Phase 1:4

056:A:Ditch southern return:cut:-:-
304:J:Same as Ditch 056 (southern return)
425:J:Same as Ditch 056 (southern return)
070:A:Ditch 056 southern return:fill:-:silty
clay
071:A:Ditch 056 southern return:fill:-:silty
clay
079:A:Ditch 056 southern return:fill:-:silty
clay
088:A:Ditch 056 southern return:fill:-:clay
089:A:Ditch 056 southern return:fill:-:silty
clay
159:A:Ditch 056 southern return:fill:-:silty
clay
160:A:Ditch 056 southern return:fill:-:silty
clay
161:A:Ditch 056 southern return:fill:-:silty
clay
162:A:Ditch 056 southern return:fill:-:silty
clay
163:A:Ditch 056 southern return:fill:-:silty
clay
164:A:Ditch 056 southern return:fill:-:clay

165:A:Ditch 056 southern return:fill:-:clay
166:A:Ditch 056 southern return:fill:-:silty
clay
305:J:Ditch 056 southern return:fill:-:bulk
removal
469:N:Ditch 056 southern return:fill:-:clay
471:N:Ditch 056 southern return:fill:-:clay
472:N:Ditch 056 southern return:fill:-:silt
473:N:Ditch 056 southern return:fill:-
:sandy silt
474:N:Ditch 056 southern return:fill:-:clay
475:N:Ditch 056 southern return:fill:-:clay
476:N:Ditch 056 southern return:fill:-:silty
clay

553:A:Re-cut 056:cut: gully:-
010:A: Same as 553
011:A:Re-cut 553:fill:-:silty clay
057:A:Re-cut 553:fill:-:silty clay

426:N:Pit:cut
427:N:Pit 426:fill:-:loamy clay
436:N:Pit:cut:-
422:N:Same as 436
437:N:Pit 436:fill:-:sandy clay

434:N:Pit:cut:-
435:N:Pit 434:fill:-:sandy clay

458:N:Pit:cut:-
462:N:Pit 458:fill:-:silty clay
463:N:Pit 458:fill:-:clay
483:N:Pit 458:fill:-:clay

369:N:Latrine pit?:cut:-:-
392:N:Latrine pit 369:fill:-:clay
393:N:Latrine pit 369:fill:-:organic sandy
clay
394:N:Latrine pit 369:fill:-:clay
395:N:Latrine pit 369:fill:-:organic silty clay
396:N:Latrine pit 369:fill:-:organic silty clay
397:N:Latrine pit 369:fill:-: silty clay
398:N:Latrine pit 369:fill:-:organic silty clay
399:N:Latrine pit 369:fill:-:clay
400:N:Latrine pit 369:fill:-:organic silty clay
401:N:Latrine pit 369:fill:-:gritty sand
438:N:Latrine pit 369:fill:-:organic silty clay
439:N:Latrine pit 369:fill:-:sandy silt
493:N:Latrine pit 369:fill:-:silty clay

Phase 1:5

386:N:Destruction layer:-:clay
464:N:Same as 386
387:N:Destruction layer:-:-:charcoal
388:N:Destruction layer:-:-:sandy clay
465:N:Destruction layer:-:-:silty clay
466:N:Same as 465
467:N:Destruction layer:-:-:silty clay
468:N:Destruction layer:-:-:clay
470:N:Destruction layer:-:-:silty clay
494:N:Destruction layer:-:-:silty clay

Phase 2.1

140:C: Ditch signal station/fortlet southern
return:cut:-:-
231:G:Same as 140 (eastern return)
543:U:Same as 140 (western return)
141:C:Ditch 140 signal station/
fortlet southern return:fill:-:silty sand
142:C:Ditch 140 signal station/fortlet
southern return:fill:-:sand

143:C:Ditch 140 signal station/fortlet southern return:fill:-:clay
144:C:Ditch 140 signal station/fortlet southern return:fill:-:sandy clay
145:C:Ditch 140 signal station/fortlet southern return:fill:-:silty sand
146:C:Ditch 140 signal station/fortlet southern return:fill:-:clay
147:C:Ditch 140 signal station/fortlet southern return:fill:-:silty clay
148:C:Ditch 140 signal station/fortlet southern return:fill:-:silty clay
149:C:Ditch 140 signal station/fortlet southern return:fill:-:silty clay
150:C:Ditch 140 signal station/fortlet southern return:fill:-:silty clay
151:C:Ditch 140 signal station/fortlet southern return:fill:-:silty clay
152:C:Ditch 140 signal station/fortlet southern return:fill:-:clay
153:C:Ditch 140 signal station/fortlet southern return:fill:-:silty clay
154:C:Ditch 140 signal station/fortlet southern return:fill:-:sandy clay
155:C:Ditch 140 signal station/ fortlet southern return:fill:-:silty clay
156:C:Ditch 140 signal station/fortlet southern return:fill:-:silty clay
157:C:Ditch 140 signal station/fortlet southern return:fill:-:silty clay
232:G:Ditch 140 signal station/fortlet eastern return:fill:-:organic
233:G:Ditch 140 signal station/fortlet eastern return:fill:-:silty clay
234:G:Ditch 140 signal station/fortlet eastern return:fill:-:organic
235:G:Ditch 140 signal station/fortlet eastern return:fill:-:clay

118:C:Stakehole:cut/fill:-:-
119:C:Stakehole:cut/fill::silty clay
120:C:Stakehole:cut/fill:-:silty clay
121:C:Stakehole:cut/fill:-:silty clay
122:C:Stakehole:cut/fill:-:silty clay
123:C:Stakehole:cut/fill:-:silty clay
124:C:Stakehole:cut/fill:-:silty clay
125:C:Stakehole:cut/fill:-:silty clay
126:C:Stakehole:cut/fill:-:silty clay

267:G:Posthole:cut:-:-
266:G:Posthole 267:fill:posthole:sandy silt
289:G:Posthole:cut:-:-
290:G:Posthole 289:fill:-:clay
291:G:Posthole:cut:-:-
292:G:Posthole:cut:-:-
293:G:Posthole:cut:-:-

Phase 2.2

221:G:Ditch, re-cut of 140:cut:-:-
222:G:Re-cut 221:fill:-:organic
263:G:Re-cut 221:fill:-:silty clay

265:G:Ditch:cut:-:-
264:G:Ditch 265:fill:-:organic

194:C:Ditch/foundation trench southern return:cut:-:-
236:G:Same as 194 (eastern return)
544:U:Same as 194 (western return)
189:C:Ditch/foundation trench 194 southern return:fill:-:silty clay
190:C:Ditch/foundation trench 194 southern return:fill:-:silty clay
191:C:Ditch/foundation trench 194 0 southern return:fill:-:silty clay

192:C:Ditch/foundation trench 194 southern return:fill:-:silty clay
193:C:Ditch/foundation trench 194 southern return:fill:-:silty clay
237:G:Ditch/foundation trench 194 eastern return:fill:-:silty clay
238:G:Ditch/foundation trench 194 eastern return:fill:-:silty clay
239:G:Ditch/foundation trench 194 eastern return:fill:-:silty clay
240:G:Ditch/foundation trench 194 eastern return:fill:-:sandy clay
260:G:Ditch/foundation trench 194 eastern return:fill:-:silty clay
261:G:Ditch/foundation trench 194 eastern return:fill:-:silty clay

513:T:Outwork/*titulus* ditch:cut:-:-
517:T:Outwork/*titulus* ditch 513:fill:-:clay
518:T:Outwork/*titulus* ditch 513:fill::silt

424:N:Pit:cut:-:-
479:N:Pit 424:fill:-:sandy silt
480:N:Pit 424:fill:-:silty clay
481:N:Pit 424:fill:-:clay
482:N:Pit 424:fill:-:organic
495:N:Pit 424:fill:-:clay

457:N:Pit:cut:-:-
484:N:Pit 457:fill:-:silty clay

368:N:Pit:cut:-:-
389:N:Same as 368
379:N:Pit 368:fill:-:silty clay
380:N:Pit 368:fill:-:clay
381:N:Pit 368:fill:-:silty clay
382:N:Pit 368:fill:-:silt
383:N:Pit 368:fill:-:sandy silt
390:N:Same as 379-383 bulk removal
391:N:Same as 379-383 bulk removal

370:N:Pit:cut:-:-
402:N:Pit 370:fill:-:sandy silty clay
403:N:Pit 370:cut:-:-
404:N:Pit 370:fill:-:silty clay
405:N:Pit 370:fill:-:silty clay

367:N:Pit:cut:-:-
372:N:Pit 367:fill:-:silty clay
373:N:Pit 367:fill:-:sandy clay
374:N:Pit 367:fill:-:silty clay
375:N:Pit 367:fill:-:silty clay
376:N:Pit 367:fill:-:silty clay
377:N:Pit 367:fill:-:clay
378:N:Pit 367:fill:-:sand

477:N.Destruction? layer:-:-:clay
478:N.Destruction? layer:-:-:silty clay

Phase 3.1

075:C:Rampart revetment:-:-:sandstone
077:C:Rampart revetment:tumble:-:sandstone
117:C:Rampart revetment foundation trench:-:cut:-:-
288:G:Same as 117
076:C:Rampart revetment footings:-:cobbles
276:G:Same as 076
078:C:Rampart turves:-:-:clay
301:G:Same as 078

306:G:Same as 078
317:G:Rampart layer:-:gritty sand
318:G:Rampart layer:-:silt
319:G:Rampart layer:-:clay
320:G:Rampart layer:-:clay

294:G:Wall or inner rampart
revetment:-:cobbles
277:G:Wall or inner revetment
tumble:-:cobbles
295:G:Surface:-:-:pebble

220:G:Ditch sandstone fort eastern
return:cut:-:-
322:C:Same as 220 (southern return)
408:P:Same as 220 (southern return)
456:Q:Same as 220 (southern return)
546:U:Same as 220 (southern return)
219:G:Ditch 220 sandstone fort eastern
return:fill:-:silty clay
331:C:Ditch 220 sandstone fort southern
return:fill:-:sandy clay
332:C:Ditch 220 sandstone fort southern
return:fill:-:clay
333:C:Ditch 220 sandstone fort southern
return:fill:-:clay
409:P:Ditch 220 sandstone fort southern
return:fill:-:silty clay
410:P:Ditch 220 sandstone fort southern
return:fill:-:clay loam
490:Q:Ditch 220 sandstone fort southern
return:fill:-:silty clay
492:Q:Ditch 220 sandstone fort southern
return:fill:-:silt

538:S:Outwork ditch:cut:-:-
539:S:Outwork ditch 538:fill:-:sandy silt
540:S:Outwork ditch 538:fill:-:sandy clay
541:S:Outwork ditch 538:fill:-:organic
542:S:Outwork ditch 538:fill:-:sand

359:N:Annexe ditch:cut:-:-
360:N:Annexe ditch 359:fill:-:clay
361:N:Annexe ditch 359:fill:-:clay
362:N:Annexe ditch 359:fill:-:organic

299:G:Hollow:cut:-:-
300:G:Hollow 299:fill:-:silty sand

172:C:Linear feature:cut:-:-
167:C:Linear feature 172:fill:-:silty clay
168:C:Linear feature 172:fill:-:silt and
gravel
169:C:Linear feature 172:fill:-:silty clay
170:C:Linear feature 172:fill:-:silt and
gravel
171:C:Linear feature 172:fill:-:silty clay

Phase 3.2

218:G:Ditch first re-cut of 220 eastern
return:cut:-:-
323:C:Same as 218 (southern return)
411:P:Same as 218 (southern return)
487:Q:Same as 218 (southern return)
545:U:Same as 218 (southern return)
215:G:Ditch 218 eastern return:fill:-:silty
clay
216:G:Ditch 218 eastern return:fill:-:silty
clay
217:G:Ditch 218 eastern return:fill:-:silty
clay
327:C:Ditch 218 southern return:fill:-:sandy
clay
328:C:Ditch 218 southern return:fill:-:clay
329:C:Ditch 218 southern return:fill:-:clay

330:C:Ditch 218 southern return:fill:-:silty
clay
344:C:Ditch 218 southern return:fill:-
:cobble
412:P:Ditch 218 southern return:fill:-:silty
clay
413:P:Ditch 218 southern return:fill:-:clay
loam
488:Q:Ditch 218 southern return:fill:-:silty
clay

534:S:Outwork ditch first re-cut of 538:cut:-
535:S:Outwork ditch 534:fill:-:sandy clay
536:S:Outwork ditch 534:fill:-:sandy clay
537:S:Outwork ditch 534:fill:-:sandy clay

352:N:Annexe ditch first re-cut of 359:cut:-
:-
353:N:Annexe ditch 352:fill:-:organic

Phase 3.3

214:G:Ditch second re-cut of 220 eastern
return:cut:-:-
324:C:Same as 214 (southern return)
421:Q:Same as 214 (southern return)
547:U:Same as 214 (southern return)
528:T: Same as 214 (southern return)
210:G:Ditch 214 eastern return:fill:-:silty
clay
211:G:Ditch 214 eastern return:fill:-:silty
clay
212:G:Ditch 214 eastern return:fill:-:sandy
clay
213:G:Ditch 214 eastern return:fill:-:silty
clay
325:C:Ditch 214 southern return:fill:-:silty
clay
326:C:Ditch 214 southern return:fill:-:silt
343:C:Ditch 214 southernreturn:fill:-:silty
clay
444:Q:Ditch 214 southern return:fill:-
:sandy clay
447:Q:Ditch 214 southern return:fill:-:clay
448:Q:Ditch 214 southern return:fill:-:silty
clay
529:T:Ditch 214:fill of 528

530:S:Outwork ditch second re-cut of
538:cut:-:-
459:S: Same as 530
486:S:Outwork ditch 530:fill:-:silty clay
531:S:Outwork ditch 530:fill:-:silty sand
532:S:Outwork ditch 530:fill:-:organic
533:S:Outwork ditch 530:fill:-:clay
485:S:Same as 533

354:N:Annexe ditch second re-cut of
359:cut:-:-
355:N:Annexe ditch 354:fill:-:silty clay
356:N:Annexe ditch 354:fill:-:clay
357:N:Annexe ditch 354:fill:-:clay and
gravel
358:N:Annexe ditch 354:fill:-:organic

371:N:Ditch:cut:-:-
384:N:Ditch 371:fill:-:silty clay
385:N:Ditch 371:fill:-:silty clay

Phase 2/3 Extramural activity

429:M:Industrial hollow:cut:-:-
418:M:Industrial hollow 429:fill:-:silty clay
420:M:Industrial hollow 429:fill:-:silty clay

430:M:Industrial hollow 429:fill:-:clay
431:M:Industrial hollow 429:fill:-:silty clay

442:M:Hearth?:cut:-:-
440:M:Hearth? 440:fill:-:silty clay
441:M:Hearth? 440:fill:-:sandy clay silt

433:M:Ditch:cut:-:-
449:M:Ditch 443:fill:-:silty clay
450:M:Ditch 443:fill:-:clay

417:M:Wall footings:-:-:cobbles
554:M:Foundation trench: cut:-:-
419:M:Fill :-:-:sandy clay
428:M:Wall tumble:-:-:cobble
443:M:Layer:-:-:industrial material

406:M:Linear feature:cut:-:-
407:M:Linear feature 406:fill:-:silty clay

414:M:Linear feature:cut:-:-
415:M:Linear feature 414:fill:-:silty clay
416:M:Linear feature 414:fill:-:silty clay

366:L:Road surface?:-:-:pebble
345:L:Ditch:cut:-:-
346:L:Ditch 345:fill:-:sandy clay

335:H:Road surface?:-:-:pebble
303:H:Layer:-:-:silty clay
334:H:Same as 303

340:H:Metalled surface?:-:-:clay silt
341:H:Metalled surface?:-:-:sandy silt

133:D:Layer:-:-:boulder
134:D:Layer:-:-:clay
138:D:Linear feature:cut:-:-
139:D:Layer:-:-:silty clay loam
158:D:Surface?:-:-:pebble
204:D:Surface?:-:-:pebble
207:D:Surface?:-:-:pebble

268:D:Layer:-:-:sandy silt
269:D:Posthole:cut:-:-
270:D:Posthole 269:fill:-:silty clay
271:D:Posthole 269:fill:-:silty clay

048:A:Feature:cut:-:-
049:A:Feature 048:fill:-:silty clay
050:A:Feature:cut:-:-
051:A:Feature 050:fill:-:silty clay
054:A:Feature:cut:-:-
055:A:Feature 054:fill:-:silty clay
085:A:Layer:-:-:pebble
130:A:Feature:cut:-:-
131:A:Feature 130:fill:-:sandy clay
018:A:Linear feature:cut: :-
019:A:Linear feature 018:fill:-:silty clay
020:A:Linear feature:cut:-:-
021:A:Linear feature 020:fill:-:silty clay
187:A:Linear feature:cut:-:-
188:A:Linear feature 187:fill:-:clay loam

296:H:Pit:cut:-:-
297:H:Pit 296:fill:-:clay loam

496:R:Pit:cut:-:-
497:R:Pit 496:fill:-:silt

516:T:Linear feature:cut:-:-
519:T:Linear feature 516:fill:-:siltyclay

008:A:Linear feature:cut:-:-
009:A:Linear feature 008:fill:-silty clay
106:A:Posthole:cut:-:-
107:A:Posthole 106:fill:-:silty clay
044:A:Linear feature:cut:-:-

045:A:Linear feature 044:fill:-:silty clay
040:A:Hollow:cut:-:-
041:A:Hollow 040:fill:-: charcoal
025:A:Hollow:cut:-:-
026:A:Hollow 025:fill:-:silty clay

094:A:Linear feature:cut:-:-
095:A:Linear feature 094:fill:-:clay
096:A:Linear feature:cut:-:-
097:A:Linear feature 096:fill:-:sandy clay
030:A:Hollow:cut:-:-
031:A:Hollow 030:fill:-:clayey sand
072:A:Hollow 030:fill:-:pebble
086:A:Posthole:cut:-:-
087:A:Posthole 086:fill::silty loam

046:A:Linear feature:cut:-:-
047:A:Linear feature 046:fill:-:silty clay
073:A:Linear feature:cut:-:-
074:A:Linear feature 073:fill:-:siltyclay

280:F:Pit:cut:-:-
279:F:Pit 279:fill:-:organic

522:V:Posthole:cut:-:-
521:V:Posthole 521:fill:-:sandy clay
524:V:Linear feature:cut:-:-
523:V:Linear feature 524:fill:-:silty clay
526:V:Linear feature:cut:-:-
525:V:Linear feature 526:fill:-:siltyclay

548:W:Linear feature:cut/fill:-:-

551:Z:Linear feature:cut:-:-
552:Z:Linear feature 551:fill:-:silty clay

Phase 4 Possible medieval features

445:Q:Linear feature:cut:ditch:-
423:Q: Same as 445
446:Q:Linear feature
445:fill:ditch:clay loam
453:Q:Posthole:cut:-:-
454:Q:Posthole 453:fill:-:silty clay
455:Q:Spread:-:-:pebble
460:S:Ditch:cut:-:-
461:S:Ditch 460:fill:-:silty sand

Other/modern features/layers

001/002/003/027/132/223/432:Layer:
subsoil:loam
028/029/203:Layer:-:subsoil:silty clay
127/128/278/287/307/321/452/451:
Cleaning layer

035:A:Tree disturbance:-:-:-
036:A:Tree disturbance 035:fill:-:silt
104:A:Linear feature:cut:-:-
105:A:Linear feature 104:fill:-:silty clay

241:B:Linear feature:cut:-:-
242:B:Linear feature 241:fill:-:silty clay
243:B:Linear feature:cut:-:-
244:B:Linear feature 243:fill:-:silty clay
245:B:Posthole:cut:-:-
246:B:Posthole 245:fill:-:silty loam
247:B:Linear feature:cut:-:-
248:B:Linear feature 247:fill:-:silty clay
249:B:Linear feature:cut:-:-
250:B:Linear feature 249:fill:-:silty clay
251:B:Linear feature:cut:-:-
252:B:Linear feature 251:fill:sandy clay
253:B:Posthole:cut and fill:-:-

274:B:Linear feature:cut:-:-
275:B:Linear feature 274:fill:-:silty clay

181:C:Pit:cut:-:-
173:C:Pit 181:fill:-:silty clay
174:C:Pit 181:fill:-:silty clay
175:C:Pit 181:fill:-:silty clay
176:C:Pit 181:fill:-:sandy gravel
177:C:Pit 181:fill:-:silty clay
178:C:Pit 181:fill:-:silty gravel
179:C:Pit 181:fill:-:gravelly clay
180:C:Pit 181:fill:-:silty clay
186:C:Pit:cut:-:-
182:C:Pit 186:fill:-:silty clay
183:C:Pit 186:fill:-:silty clay
184:C:Pit 186:fill:-:clay
185:C:Pit 186:fill:-:silty clay

272:D:Tree disturbance:cut:-:-
273:D:Tree disturbance 272:fill:-:sandy silt

284:H:Ditch:cut:-:-
285:H:Ditch 284:fill:-:sand
286:H:Ditch 284:fill:-:clay

350:H:Feature:cut:-:-
351:H:Feature 350:fill:-:clay loam

500:T:Layer:-:-:silty clay
506:T:Layer:-:redeposited natural:clay
501:T:Linear feature:cut:-:-
503:T:Linear feature 501:fill:-:silty clay
505:T:Linear feature 501:fill:-:clay
502:T:Linear feature:cut:-:-
504:T:Linear feature 502:fill:-:silty clay
507:T:Layer:-:-:pebble
508:T:Layer:-:-:silty clay
512:T:Same as 508
509:T:Layer:-:-:silty clay
510:T:Layer:-:-:pebble
511:T:Layer:-:-:silty clay
514:T:Linear feature:cut:-:-
515:T:Linear feature 514:fill:-:sandy clay
527:T:Modern drain:cut/fill:-:mixed

549:W:Layer:-:-:cobbles
550:W:Layer:-:-:sand

APPENDIX 2
FINDS CATALOGUES

Catalogue of Decorated Samian Vessels
J Mills

The first line of each entry gives: - production centre (fabric), vessel form, sherd type/s

1. Les Martres-de-Veyre, Dr 37, rim (Fig. 9.7)
Very eroded sherd with a little slip remaining on the exterior surface only. The 'ovolo' is a simple row of rings, perhaps between bead rows. This ovolo was used by potter X-13 (Stansfield and Simpson 1990, figs 45, 521, 522, 524, 525, 527), and is also used on at least one bowl from Usk (Johns 1993, figs 99, 169 and 172). The extant decoration is very faint, leaves can be seen, perhaps acanthus (Rogers 1974, K2), which were used by potter X-13 and several others. The ovolo band is pierced by a rivet with some lead remaining *in situ*. Lead can also be seen infilling a small crack in the interior of the bowl.
Date: Trajanic
256/1193, Phase 1.1

2. La Graufesenque, Dr 29, body
Eroded with only a little slip remaining on the exterior surface. The upper and lower zones are separated by a wide, plain band above the carination, with bead rows above and below it. In the upper zone the extant decoration comprises a plant of five unevenly spaced 'leaves' with a bar below. Two figures can be seen in the lower zone; to the left Hermet 1934, pl 18.42, and to the right Hermet 1934, pl 19.80.
Date AD 75-85
24/1031, Phase 1:2

3. Lezoux, Dr 37, rim
The decoration is panelled, with the panels divided by bead rows. Full-length panels alternate with ones containing an inhabited, double-bordered festoon above a figure. The individual poinçons are not readily recognisable because the external surface is heavily eroded. The panel on the left, however, contains a very abraded seated Apollo (Oswald 1936-7, O.83), with rings as an infill beneath. In the central panel the head and shoulders of panther O.1542 (*ibid*) are used below the festoon, and in the far right panel there is a standing figure of similar size and stance to O.636 and O.639 (*ibid*), although it is not necessarily either. It is difficult to attribute this piece, but it seems likely that it was the work of Attianus rather than of one of his associates. Attianus certainly used half-animals, as can be seen on bowls from Alchester and Verulamium (Stansfield and Simpson 1990, pl 85.1 and 12). The scheme of alternating panels can be seen on a bowl of his from Corbridge (Stansfield and Simpson 1990, pl 85.10), although with vegetative and geometric motifs rather than human figures in the large panels. Similarly, the combination of rings with the seated Apollo occurs on a stamped bowl from Birdoswald (Stansfield and Simpson 1990, pl 86.20).
Date: Hadrianic/early Antonine

136/1121, Phase 1:2

4. La Graufesenque, Dr 37, rim
Very eroded exterior surface, but some elements of the design can be discerned. The ovolo has a rosette terminal to the tongue, and there is a wreath below. The figures include a crouched lion (Hermet 1934, pl 25.15) with a *Bestiarius* (Hermet 1934, pl 24.289) to the left.
Date: Flavian
229/1169, Phase 1:2

5. La Graufesenque, Dr 37, body
Very eroded. The ovolo has a trifid end to the tongue, which bends to the left; this was used by several potters from La Graufesenque, including Albanus, Amandus, Bassinus, and Litugenus. There is a wavy line beneath the ovolo. A small area of panelled design survives, with a dog to the right. Panels are divided by a vertical bead row. An elongated serrated leaf can also be seen.
Date: AD 80-110
229/3059, Phase 1:2

6. La Graufesenque, Dr 29 or 37, body (Fig 9.3)
The borders of two medallions or festoons are visible. A pendant four-lobed leaf between them is also seen on a bowl from Wilderspool stamped Sulpicus. Below this is a pair of backward-looking birds, perhaps O.2248 and O.2293 (Oswald 1936-7).
Date: Flavian or Flavian/Trajanic
230/1178, Phase 1:2

7. La Graufesenque, Dr 29, body (Fig 9.2)
This is a small example for this form. The decorative scheme in the upper zone has a hare running to the right (Oswald 1936-7, O.2074), and the lower zone includes a pair of gladiators (*ibid*, O.1020 and O.1021) with a leaf between them. The border between the upper and lower zone is a broad, plain band with a wavy line above and below it. Both the gladiators and the hare are known from bowls stamped M Crestio (Knorr 1952, Taf 52). His bowls, however, have bead rows and not wavy lines flanking the band between the zones.
Date: AD 75-85
338/1268, Phase 1:2

8. Lezoux (fabric more orange than is normal for Lezoux), Dr 37, body (Fig 9.12)
The external surface is worn/eroded, and the interior etched, deeply in some areas. A single incomplete ovolo survives, probably Rogers B35 (1974), with a bead row below. The decoration comprises double-winding scrolls with vine leaf (*ibid*, H43,) and a flapping goose (Oswald 1936-7, O.2312). The leaf is ascribed to potters X-5 and X-6; and the ovolo is that of X-6, this is thus likely to be his work.
Date AD 125-50
11/1039, Phase 1:4

9. La Graufesenque, Dr 37, body
Double-bordered ovolo with tongue to the right. The tongue has an irregular trifid end.

The border below is abraded and it is not clear whether it was a wavy line or a bead row. This ovolo was used by potters working in the style of Germanus.
Date: AD 85-110
11/3009, Phase 1:4

10. Lezoux, Dr 37, body/footring (Fig 9.11)
A wide, shallow bowl broken across the ovolo, which, although worn, may be Rogers B14 (1974), of Sacer and potter X-13, with a bead row below. The free-style decoration comprises a tree (ibid, N7), with, to the left, the hind legs and tail of a ?lion; and to the right, the raised paws of another beast, perhaps a bear. The tree was used by Attianus (AD 130-160) and Sacer (AD 125-150). Together the ovolo and tree suggest that this was the work of Sacer.
Date: AD 125-150
57/1061, Phase 1:4

11. La Graufesenque, Dr 37, body (Fig 9.5)
The ovolo is damaged, but the tongue has a trifid end. The upper and lower zones of decoration are separated by a narrow band, or perhaps a poorly moulded wavy line or bead row. The upper zone comprises a hound (Oswald 1936–7, O.1994) running to the left, with grass sprigs below and in front. On the opposite side of the hound there is a sprig of vegetation with a long slender leaf. The lower zone comprises a scroll inhabited by a bird (ibid, O.2247) and a small rosette above a wavy line. To the right, the vegetation sprig includes a triangular leaf.
Date: AD 85-110
57/3017, Phase 1:4

12. La Graufesenque, Dr 37, body (Fig 9.4)
The decoration is very worn/eroded. The ovolo is eroded, making identification impossible. The decoration is panelled, each panel bordered with wavy lines with rosettes at the junctions. The long panel contains a leafy tree with a bird, possibly O.2267 (Oswald 1936–7), perched atop it. The lower panels on either side contain festoons. Sitting stag O.1746 (ibid) is the only figure visible in the upper panels. The stag and the tree can be seen together on a bowl stamped OF SECUND (Knorr 1919, Taf 74, D) but both the stag and the bird are known from bowls stamped by a number of potters. The style of decoration is, however, typical of later Southern Gaulish vessels.
Date: AD 85-110 (Flavian - Trajanic)
57/3018, Phase 1:4

13. La Graufesenque, Dr 37, body
A fragment of panelled decoration with a corner rosette. The remaining panel fragment is infilled with parallel lines.
Date: Flavian or Flavian/Trajanic
57/3027, Phase 1:4

14. Les Martres-de-Veyre, Dr 37, body (Fig 9.8)
A well-preserved sherd with fragmentary double-bordered ovolo, the tongue ending in a pierced rosette (Rogers 1974, B7), with a crisp wavy line below. The decoration comprises a fragment of vine medallion with a bird (Rogers 1974, M10), and grape bunch (Rogers 1974, M39). The medallions and grapes are seen on several bowls from Les Martres (Terisse 1968, pl XLII, 212b, 216, 224,

225). All of the elements of the design can be attributed to potter X-13 (Donnavcvs).
Date: Trajanic
79/1079, Phase 1:4

15. Pre-export Lezoux, Dr 37, rim (Fig 9.9)
The slip is almost all gone, and it is pierced by a rivet hole. There is a double-bordered ovolo, the tongue ending in a rosette, with wavy lines below. The surviving panelled decoration is divided by bead rows, and there is a ?nine-petalled rosette below the ovolo. An almost complete panel contains a sea-monster, with acanthus tips repeated below it. The panel beneath this is incomplete, but contains a row of circles. The sea-monster is not listed by Oswald (1936-7) but is exactly paralleled on a bowl from London (Stansfield and Simpson 1990, pl 39.460) attributed to potter X-12. The fabric of the Kirkham sherd is usually associated with Les Martres-de-Veyre, but this piece might suggest that potter X-12 moved from there to Lezoux before the beginning of the main export period (c AD 120).
Date: AD 100-120
371/1291, Phase 3:3

16. La Graufesenque, Dr 37, body
The double-bordered ovolo is incomplete, but appears to have the tongue attached to the right, with a rosette terminal. It is probably the ovolo of the later Paullus of La Graufesenque (Knorr 1919, Taf 65.9). It is not clear if there was a bead row or a wavy line below it. Large rosettes below the ovolo are associated with ?wavy dividing lines. The only clear element of the decoration is a deeply folded tendril and a pendant leaf.
Date: AD 75-100
371/3037, Phase 3:3

17. La Graufesenque, Dr 30/37, rim
The same ovolo as 12, but not from the same bowl. There is a wavy line beneath. The surface is eroded and, in the plain zone below the rim, there is a deep groove which was made prior to firing.
Date: AD 75-110
371/3038, Phase 3:3

18. Lezoux, Dr 37, body
Fragment of a bead row, with panther O.1536 (Oswald 1936–7), and snake and rock ornament (ibid, O.2155) in the ground above. Both motifs were used by Criciro (AD 125-165, Stansfield and Simpson 1990, pl 118.17) and Attianus (AD 125-145, Stansfield and Simpson 1990, pl 86.15).
Date: 125-165
212/1113, Phase 3:3

19. La Graufesenque, Dr 37, rim, body and base (Fig 9.1)
Four sherds from a single vessel, not all joining. The bowl is finely potted. The decoration comprises a tree or trees with pendant grape bunches. One sherd has the feet of an unknown figure on one side of a tree, and a leopard above a hillock or tuft of vegetation on the other. Hermet (1934, pl 100.12) shows the tree and the backward-looking leopard together. There is no ovolo. The style is that of Germanus of La Graufesenque.
Date: AD 70-85
371/3036, 355/3078, 3079, 3083, Phase 3:3

20. La Graufesenque, Dr 37, body
Thick eroded body sherd. The lower part of the decoration comprises two heavy, corded festoons, one with a spiral ending in a rosette, the other with backward-looking bird O.2290 or O.2291 (Oswald 1936–7). The upper limit of the zone is marked by a bead row. The festoons are linked, with a simple tassel between. This design seems to be repeated. There is no basal wreath, but a line, possibly a degenerate bead row, defines the lower edge of the decoration. A similar style was used by many Flavian and Trajanic potters, and can be seen on a bowl by Biragillus from Carlisle (Dickinson 1990, fig 181.47).
Date: AD 80-110
355/3080, Phase 3:3

21. La Graufesenque, Dr 37, body
Only the lowest part of the decoration remains, comprising an incomplete basal wreath of reverse S-shaped gadroons, with an abraded bead row above. Small parts of two panels remain, one with the feet of a gladiator (Hermet 1934, pl 21.140) and perhaps another; the other contains a St Andrew's cross with triple poppy heads.
Date AD 80-100
355/3081, Phase 3:3

22. La Graufesenque, Dr 37, body
Only the lowest part of the decoration remains, comprising an incomplete basal wreath with an abraded bead row above. Other elements include a grass tuft. The wreath was used by Mercator and his associates.
Date: AD 85-110
355/3082, Phase 3:3

23. Les Martres-de-Veyre, Dr 37, body
A very small sherd, with finely moulded decoration; only a small bead row, and a double-bordered ?medallion remain.
Date: Trajanic/Hadrianic
533/3084, Phase 3:3

24. Lezoux, Dr 37, body (Fig 9.10)
Almost half of the vessel wall survives, but the ovolo, rim and base are missing. The main decorative scheme is alternating festoons and arcades of wreath (Rogers 1974, F8), bordered top and bottom by a bead row. Two of the spaces so created are further divided into two by a bead row. From left to right the decoration comprises boar O.1668 (Oswald 1936–7) with, below, a pair of hares (ibid, O.2057 and O.2117(?)) facing each other; a pair of sphinxes (ibid, O.854 and O.857), with a triton (ibid, O.18) below; and dancer O.361 (ibid). A filling a whole festoon. This last festoon is slightly angular, and shows some contraction of the design in order to fit it in the space available. At the far right a very small part of another arcaded panel can be seen, containing a ?club, or ?lion's tail. Three rosettes (Rogers 1974, C280) can be seen just below the uppermost bead row. The left arm of the triton is incomplete, and this can be seen, again used after the poinçon broke, on a bowl of potter X-13 from London (Stansfield and Simpson 1990, pl 45.525). The general style of the design can be compared with stamped bowls of Attianus (Stansfield and Simpson 1990, pl 87. 20, and .26). The latter shows the wreath

to form the scroll). The work is that of the Sacer group, but perhaps has more in common with Attianus than others of this group.
Date: AD 125-145
533/1369, Phase 3:3

25. La Graufesenque, Dr 37, body (Fig 9.6)
Eroded interior and decoration. The decoration is divided into upper and lower zones by a ?degenerate bead row. The lower zone may be decorated with a winding scroll, but only an unusual form of spiral and a long tassel are visible. The upper zone may have contained festoons.
Date: Late Flavian or Trajanic
31/1050, Phase 2/3

26. Les Martres-de-Veyre, Dr 30 or 37, rim
Badly eroded, only a fragment of the double-bordered ovolo survives.
Date: Trajanic
31/3042, Phase 2/3

27. La Graufesenque, Dr 37, rim
All surfaces and edges are very eroded. The ovolo is double-bordered, the tongue swells at the end, but no further detail is visible. There is a wavy line below the ovolo. The only other surviving decoration is a vertical wavy line between linked festoons.
Date: Flavian
72/3048, Phase 2/3

28. Les Martres-de-Veyre, Dr 37, body
Very eroded, ovolo barely visible, tongue attached to the left.
Date: Trajanic
72/3049, Phase 2;3

29. Lezoux, Dr 37, body
Two sherds. The exterior of the larger fragment (133/1125) is very eroded, with no slip remaining on the decoration, although the interior is only slightly pitted; the smaller sherd is slightly burnt. The double-bordered ovolo is incomplete and not identifiable. It has a wavy line below. The free-style decoration is slightly crowded. It comprises dolphins (Oswald 1936–7, O.2394), a lion, and a ?running/leaping beast, neither of which are clear or complete enough for identification. The ribs at the bottom of the decorated zone are typical of the work of potter X-6. There is a simple basal wreath with, beneath it, a raised band between two narrow ridges.
Date: AD 125-150
133/1125, 139/1146, Phase 2/3

30. Lezoux, Dr 37, body
Fragment of basal wreath with a plain band beneath. Typical of potter X-6. Burnt. Not the same vessel as 18.
Date: AD 125-150
139/3056, Phase 2/3

31. La Graufesenque, Dr 37, body
Only the lower part of the ovolo survives; the tongue has a trifid end. There is an abraded bead row beneath, and the decoration is divided horizontally by a ?bead row. A right-facing lion (Oswald 1936–7, O.1418) is all that remains of the upper zone/panel. An incomplete festoon inhabited by backward-facing bird O.2248 (ibid) survives below it.
Date: AD 80-110

287/1207, Modern

32. La Graufesenque, ?DR 37, body
Eroded body sherd, the only decoration remaining being a row of sword-like leaves.
Date: Flavian
287/3089, Modern

33. La Graufesenque, Dr 37, base
Only the lowest part of the design survives, comprising a medallion and a row of sword-shaped leaves. Not the same bowl as 32.
Date: Flavian
287/3090, Modern

34. La Graufesenque, Dr 37, rim
Single-bordered ovolo, slightly smudged, with a straight tongue to the left. The tongue end is a small pierced circle attached slightly to the left. Beneath is a wavy line and a wreath of chevrons, and traces of a second wavy line can be detected below the wreath. The chevron is an early type.
Date: AD 70-85
287/3093, Modern

35. Les Martres-de-Veyre, Dr 37, body
Incomplete ovolo with bead row beneath. The ovolo may be Rogers B20 (1974).
Date: Trajanic
451/3100, Modern

36. La Graufesenque, Dr 37, base/footring
A single grass tuft is all that remains of the decoration.
Date: Flavian/Trajanic
451/3102, Modern

Catalogue of the Copper Alloy Artefacts
C Howard-Davis

1. Approximately half of the bow of a Colchester derivative-type brooch, foot, pin and spring missing. Bow decorated, distinctive mouldings either side of the bow, at the head, suggests a Polden Hill type, late first or early second century. Medium condition, incomplete.
L: 32mm; Th: 11mm
276/1116/1, Phase 3.1

2. Half of a silvered button. Medium condition, incomplete.
L: 27mm; Th: 2mm
003/1007/1, Modern

3. Two fragments of copper pipe. Medium condition, heavily corroded, incomplete.
L: 270mm
287/1214/2, Modern

4. Small fragment of bow brooch, only spring survives, bow, pin and headloop missing. Poor condition, very incomplete.
L: 13mm; Th: 13mm
1000/1347/1, Unstratified

Catalogue of the Ironwork
C Howard-Davis

1. One nail fragment. Poor condition, incomplete.
L: 36mm
017/1024/1, Phase 1.1

2. One nail fragment. Poor condition, incomplete.
L: 52mm
011/1047/1, Phase 1.4

3. One nail fragment. Poor condition, incomplete.
L: 42mm
011/1117/1, Phase 1.4

4. One nail fragment. Poor condition, incomplete.
L: 33mm
300/1223/1, Phase 3.1

5. One nail fragment. Poor condition, incomplete.
L: 125mm
355/1277/2, Phase 3.3

6. One very large hook or U-shaped shackle with rectangular section, possibly a cart fitting. Poor condition, almost complete.
L: 230mm
355/1333/1, Phase 3.3

7. One small fragment of strip, possibly with nail at one end. Poor condition, incomplete.
L: 57mm
533/1374/2, Phase 3.3

8. One nail fragment. Poor condition, incomplete.
L: 44mm
003/1008/1, Modern

9. Two nail fragments. Poor condition, incomplete. ?Modern.
L: 63mm; L: 100mm
287/1214/2, Modern

10. One nail fragment. Poor condition, incomplete.
L: 57mm
321/1346/2, Modern

11. One nail fragment. Good condition, almost complete. Nail with no head, shaft expands.
L: 57mm
451/1358/1, Modern

Catalogue of the Lead Artefacts
C Howard-Davis

1. Semi-circular curl of D-sectioned wire. Medium condition, incomplete.
L: 18mm; Diam: 2mm
088/1115/1, Phase 1.4

2. Irregular fragment of thin sheet, folded several times, probably scrap. Good condition, complete.
L: 72mm
431/1348/1, Phase 2/3

3. Two solidified drips. Medium condition, complete.
i) L: 30mm; W: 15mm
ii) L: 84mm; W: 15mm
451/1307/2, Modern

Catalogue of the Roman and Later Glass
C Howard-Davis

1. Two relatively large mid-pane fragments of window. Good condition, slight abrasion, incomplete. First to third centuries.
Th: 4mm
209/1158/1, Phase 1.1

2. Small blown vessel base in good colourless glass, possibly roughly grozed to form a round tally. Good condition, very incomplete. Second century.
Wall th: 1.5mm
209/1158/2, Phase 1.1

3. Small ?mould-blown vessel fragment. Good condition, very incomplete.
Wall th: 2mm
024/1035/1, Phase 1.2

4. One mid-pane fragment of window. Good condition, slight dulling, incomplete. First to third centuries.
Th: 3mm
136/1182/1, Phase 1.2

5. Six fragments vessels. Good condition, incomplete. One angular and five curving body fragments. First to third centuries.
Wall th: between 2-6 mm
229/1175/1, Phase 1.2

6. One transparent dark blue bead fragment. Probably globular. Poor condition, incomplete.
Int diam: 1.5mm; L: 3mm
007/1019/1, Phase 1.3

7. One fragment vessel with thick curving body. Good condition, very incomplete.
Wall th: 6mm
057/1067/1, Phase 1.4

8. One vessel fragment, seating for combed handle of mould-blown bottle. Good condition, slightly dulled, incomplete. First to third centuries.
371/1296/1, Phase 3.3

9. One fragment of a small frit melon bead with asymmetrical section. Medium condition, incomplete. First to second centuries?
L: 9mm
277/1201/1, Phase 3.1

10. One body fragment blown vessel. Bubbly metal. Good condition, very incomplete.
Wall th: 4mm
020/1028/1, Phase 2/3

11. One small body fragment, vessel. Good condition, dulled, very incomplete.
Wall Th: 2.5mm
045/1038/1, Phase 2/3

12. One body fragment, vessel. Good condition, very incomplete. Nineteenth century?
055/1057/1, Phase 2/3

13. One body fragment, vessel. Very bubbly metal. Good condition, incomplete. Eighteenth century.
242/1235/1, Modern

14. One mid-pane window fragment. Thin, greenish, slightly bubbly metal. Good condition, very incomplete. Eighteenth century.
Th: 2mm
278/1206/1, Modern

15. One large thick fragment, vessel, partially melted. Medium condition, incomplete.
Wall Th: 5.5mm
287/1215/1, Modern

16. One thick, curved fragment, vessel. Exterior surface very abraded, possibly base? Good condition, very incomplete.
Wall th: 8mm
307/1245/1, Modern

17. One small body fragment, vessel. Good condition, dulled, very incomplete.
Wall th: 7 mm
452/1337/1, Modern

18. One body fragment, small ?cylindrical bottle. Good condition, incomplete. Modern.
Wall th: 4mm
1000/1353/1, Unstratified

Catalogue of the Leather
C Howard-Davis

1. One fragment of folded strip, with irregular stitching along both edges. Compression suggests that it derives from a beaded gable seam, but it is rather narrow, perhaps a different beaded seam - saddle?? Good condition, incomplete.
L: 135mm; Th: 1mm
338/1313/1, Phase 1.3

2. One fragment of sheet with a short length of seam surviving. Stitches are widely spaced and irregular. The compression pattern suggests a wide overlap, possibly a beaded seam. The panel edge is untrimmed, and represents the natural hide edge. Good condition, incomplete.
L: 78mm; Th: 1mm
472/1378/1, Phase 1.4

Catalogue of the Wooden Artefacts
C Howard-Davis

1. One fragment roundwood. Poor condition, incomplete.
L: 153mm; W: 38mm; Th: 34mm
227/2065, Phase 1.3

2. Four fragments, radially split. Unworked, insect damaged, possibly charred. Poor condition, very incomplete.
L: 350-475mm; W: 35-73mm; Th:4-16mm
227/2066, Phase 1.3

3. Plank, radially split. Adze dressed surfaces. Badly charred. Poor condition, incomplete.
L: 125mm; W: 60mm; Th: 11mm
339/2055, Phase 1.3

4. One fragment, radially split. Deformed oval section. Possibly charred. Poor condition, incomplete.
L: 160mm; W: 8mm; Th: 5.5mm
472/2058, Phase 1.4

5. Plank, radially split. Fragment, neatly cut at both ends. Pierced by square hole, 9mm x 10mm (large nail?) driven diagonally through the plank, across the grain. Poor condition, incomplete?
L: 108mm; W: 70mm; Th: 20-25mm
219/2059, Phase 3.1

6. Five fragments of ?primary conversion debris. Poor condition, complete?
L: 66-650mm; W: 19-80mm; Th: 14-50mm
332/2062, Phase 3.1

7 Tent peg, tangentially split. Notch unusual. Fair condition, degraded, complete but fragmentary.
L: 602mm; W: 57mm; Th: 20mm
216/2001, Phase 3.2

8. Tent peg, tangentially split. Head missing, point deformed. Notch at 45°. Fair condition, degraded, incomplete.
L: 410mm; W: 50mm; Th: 17mm
216/2002, Phase 3.2

9. Tent peg? radially split. Head and tip of point missing, deformed. Notch very long and shallow. Fair condition, incomplete.
L: 370mm; W: 49mm; Th: 7mm
216/2003, Phase 3.2

10. Tent peg, radially split. Head and tip of point deformed. Good condition, complete.
L: 355mm; W: 32mm; Th: 22mm
216/2004, Phase 3.2

11. Tent peg, radially split. Head and tip of point deformed. Toolmarks survive. Good condition, complete.
L: 370mm; W: 32mm; Th: 25mm
216/2005, Phase 3.2

12. Tent peg, radially split. Head missing, tip of point deformed. Notch at 30°. Good condition, incomplete.
L: 428mm; W: 39mm; Th: 14mm
216/2006, Phase 3.2

13. Fragment, radially split. Good condition complete.
L: 310mm; W: 30mm; Th: 10mm
216/2007, Phase 3.2

14. Tent peg, radially split. Head and tip of point missing. Good condition, incomplete.
L: 305mm; W: 45mm; Th: 27mm
216/2008, Phase 3.2

15. Tent peg, radially split. Head missing, point deformed. Fair condition, degraded, incomplete.
L: 380mm; W: 24mm; Th: 20mm
216/2009, Phase 3.2

16. Tent peg, radially split. Head missing. Point deformed, incomplete. Fair condition.
L: 345mm; W: 43mm; Th: 30mm
216/2010, Phase 3.2

17. Tent peg, radially split. Head deformed, tip of point missing. Good condition, incomplete.

L: 450mm; W: 50mm; 29mm
216/2011, Phase 3.2

18. Tent peg? radially split. Head and tip of point missing. Notch shallow. Fair condition, degraded, incomplete.
L: 320mm; W: 47mm; Th: 17mm
216/2012, Phase 3.2

19. Tent peg, radially split. Head and tip of point missing. Fair condition, degraded, incomplete.
L: 310mm; W: 42mm; Th: 8mm
216/2013, Phase 3.2

20. Tent peg, tangentially split. Head and tip of point missing. Notch at 30°. Fair condition.
L: 270mm; W: 33mm; Th: 13mm
216/2014, Phase 3.2

21. Tent peg, tangentially split. Head missing, point deformed. Notch shallow and concave. Fair condition, some decay, incomplete.
L: 280mm; W: 47mm; Th: 18mm
216/2015, Phase 3.2

22. Tent peg, radially split? Head and point missing. Fair condition, sapwood decayed, incomplete.
L: 200mm; W: 53mm; Th: 10mm
216/2016, Phase 3.2

23. Tent peg, radially split. Head missing, point damaged. Notch shallow and concave. Good condition, incomplete.
L: 240mm; W: 47mm; Th: 23mm
216/2017, Phase 3.2

24. Tent peg? radially split. Head and point missing. Fair condition, incomplete.
L: 350mm; W: 30mm; Th: 15mm
216/2018, Phase 3.2

25. Tent peg? tangentially split. Head and point missing. Good condition, incomplete.
L: 255mm; W: 43mm; Th: 25mm
216/2019, Phase 3.2

26. Tent peg, radially split? Head only, broken at notch. Good condition, very incomplete.
L: 232mm; W: 50mm; Th: 19mm
216/2020, Phase 3.2

27. Tent peg? radially split. Head and point missing. Notch deep and concave. Good condition, incomplete.
L: 195mm; W: 30mm; Th: 20mm
216/2021, Phase 3.2

28. Tent peg, tangential conversion. Head missing, point deformed. Fair condition, incomplete.
L: 274mm; W: 19mm; Th: 13mm
216/2022, Phase 3.2

29. Small peg, radial conversion. Top and point missing. Fair condition, almost complete.
L: 130mm; W: 14mm; Th: 11mm
216/2023, Phase 3.2

30. Tent peg, radially split. Head only, deformed, broken beneath notch. Good condition, very incomplete.
L: 165mm; W: 32mm; Th: 20mm

216/2024, Phase 3.2

31. Tent peg, radially split. Head only, deformed, broken beneath notch. Poor condition, very incomplete.
L: 250mm; W: 40mm; Th: 16mm
216/2025, Phase 3.2

32. Tent peg, radially split. Part of head and point missing. Short and shallow notch. Good condition, incomplete.
L: 160mm; W: 22mm; Th: 15mm
216/2026, Phase 3.2

33. Tent peg? radially split. Head and most of point missing. Fair condition, incomplete.
L: 180mm; W: 42mm; Th: 16mm
216/2027, Phase 3.2

34. Tent peg? tangentially split. Small, only head and notch remain, deformed. Poor condition, very incomplete.
L: 38mm; W: 18mm; Th: 7mm
216/2028, Phase 3.2

35. Tent peg, radially split. Head and notch only remain. Fair condition, very incomplete.
L: 105mm; W: 43mm; Th: 10mm
216/2029, Phase 3.2

36. Tent peg, tangentially split. Head and notch only remain. Poor condition, very incomplete.
L: 110mm; W: 31mm; Th: 15mm
216/2030, Phase 3.2

37. Tent peg, radially split. Head and notch only remain, head deformed. Fair condition, very incomplete.
L: 103mm; W: 37mm; Th: 14mm
216/2031, Phase 3.2

38. Tent peg, tangentially split. Head and notch only remain, head deformed. Fair condition, very incomplete.
L: 95mm; W: 22mm; Th: 19mm
216/2032, Phase 3.2

39. Tent peg, radially split. Head and notch only remain. Good condition, very incomplete.
L: 75mm; W: 34mm; Th: 16mm
216/2033, Phase 3.2

40. Tent peg?, radially split. Head and point missing. Good condition, very incomplete.
L: 135mm; W: 38mm, Th: 17mm
216/2034, Phase 3.2

41. Tent peg, radially split. Head only. Fair condition, very incomplete.
L: 73mm; W: 28mm; Th: 12mm
216/2035, Phase 3.2

42. Tent peg, radially split. Head and notch only remain. Good condition, very incomplete.
L: 123mm; W: 33mm; Th: 16mm
216/2036, Phase 3.2

43. Tent peg, radially split. Head and notch only remain. Fair condition, very incomplete.
L: 92mm; W: 36mm; Th: 10mm
216/2037, Phase 3.2

44. Tent peg, radially split. Head missing, point deformed. Good condition, incomplete.
L: 144mm; W: 37mm; Th: 19mm
216/2038, Phase 3.2

45. Split fragments and roundwood, 38 objects represented by 78 fragments. Fair condition, very incomplete. Featureless.
Diam roundwood: 5-15mm
216/2039, Phase 3.2

46. Tent peg, radially split. Tip of point missing, otherwise undamaged. Good condition, sapwood decayed, almost complete.
L: 644mm; W: 55mm; Th: 20mm
216/2040, Phase 3.2

47. Tent peg, radially split. Top and point deformed. Long, concave notch. Fair condition, heartwood decayed, complete.
L: 981mm; W: 55mm; Th: 30mm
216/2041, Phase 3.2

48. Tent peg, radially split. Top and point deformed. Shallow notch. Good condition, complete.
L: 644mm; W: 25mm; Th: 24-28mm
216/2042, Phase 3.2

49. Tent peg, radially split. Part of head missing, point deformed. Good condition, almost complete.
L: 536mm; W: 36mm; Th: 15mm
216/2043, Phase 3.2

50. Tent peg, radially split. Head and point deformed. Notch deep and cut at 30°.Good condition, complete.
L: 604mm; W: 48mm; Th: 13mm
216/2044, Phase 3.2

51. Tent peg, tangentially split. Head and point deformed. Notch deep and cut at 30°. Good condition, complete.
L: 387mm; W: 28mm; Th: 23mm
216/2045, Phase 3.2

52. Tent peg, radially split. Point damaged, longitudinal split. Notch shallow and concave. Fair condition, incomplete.
L: 319mm; W: 32mm; Th: 8mm
216/2046, Phase 3.2

53. Tent peg, radially split. Part of head and point missing. Appears to have two notches. Good condition, incomplete.
L: 287mm; W: 36mm; Th: 15mm
216/4047, Phase 3.2

54. Tent peg, radially split. Part of head and point missing. Notch eroded. Poor condition, incomplete.
L: 596mm; W: 54mm; Th: 8-18mm
216/4048, Phase 3.2

55. Tent peg, radially split. Part of head and point missing, point deformed. Notch concave. Poor condition, incomplete.
L: 430mm; W: 70mm; Th: 32mm
216/2049, Phase 3.2

56. Tent peg, radially split. Head missing, point deformed. Poor condition, incomplete.
L: 305mm; W: 50mm; Th: 7mm
216/2050, Phase 3.2

57. Tent peg, radially split. Head and part of notch only remains. Good condition, very incomplete.
L: 295mm; W: 43mm; Th: 14mm
216/2051, Phase 3.2

58. Tent peg, radially split. Part of head and point missing. Poor condition, incomplete.
L: 307mm; W: 37mm; Th: 15-20mm
216/2052, Phase 3.2

59. Tent peg, radially split. Head missing, point deformed. Fair condition, incomplete.
L: 156mm; W: 30mm; Th: 13mm
216/2053, Phase 3.2

60. Tent peg, radially split. Part of head missing, longitudinally split, part missing. Notch shallow and concave. Fair condition, incomplete.
L: 333mm; W: 26-27mm; Th: 12mm
216/2054, Phase 3.2

61. *Pilum muralis* (Fig 11)
Approximately 1.25m in length, it has a square to rectangular section and tapers to a sharp point at both ends. A bulbous and slightly irregular handgrip, with roughly circular section, lies a little more than half way along its length. Numerous tool marks are visible on the worked surfaces. Good condition, complete.
L: 1253mm; W: 42mm; Th: 42mm
216/2060, Phase 3.2

62. Nine fragments of ?primary conversion debris. Poor condition, complete?
L: 140-590mm; W: 16-87mm; Th: 14-43mm
216/2061, Phase 3.2

63. One fragment, unworked. Knotty and twisted. Charred. Poor condition, incomplete.
L: 167mm; W: 41mm; Th: 35mm
450/2056, Phase 2/3

64. Roundwood. Poor condition, incomplete.
L: 40-201mm; W: 38-95mm; Th: 25-73mm
497/2063, Phase 2/3

65. Roundwood, unconverted bent trunk, rotted hollow. Poor condition, incomplete.
L: 960mm; W: 200mm; Th: 130mm
497/2064, Phase 2/3

66. Two poorly preserved, probably unworked fragments, radially split. Poor condition, incomplete.
L: 40mm; W: 17mm; Th: 16mm
452/2057, Modern

Plant and invertebrate remains (J Carrott, A Hall, M Issitt, H Kenward, F Large, and B McKenna)

Taxonomic order and nomenclature for plants follow Smith (1978) for mosses, Tutin et al (1964–80) ,or vascular plants. The list of plants includes parts recorded.

Mosses
Sphagnum sp(p)
    leaf/leaves/shoot fragment(s)
Leucobryum glaucum (Hedw.) Ångstr.
    leaf/leaves/shoot fragment(s)
Neckera complanata (Hedw.) Hüb.
    leaf/leaves/shoot fragment(s)
Thuidium tamariscinum (Hedw.) Br. Eur.
    leaf/leaves/shoot fragment(s)
Drepanocladus sp(p)
    leaf/leaves/shoot fragment(s)
Isothecium myosuroides Brid.
    leaf/leaves/shoot fragment(s)
Eurhynchium sp(p)
    leaf/leaves/shoot fragment(s)
Hypnum cf *cupressiforme* Hedw.
    leaf/leaves/shoot fragment(s)
Rhytidiadelphus squarrosus (Hedw.) Warnst.
    leaf/leaves/shoot fragment(s)
Pleurozium schreberi (Brid.) Mitt.
    leaf/leaves/shoot fragment(s)
Hylocomium splendens (Hedw.) Br. Eur.
    leaf/leaves/shoot fragment(s)

Vascular plants
Filicales (fern)
    pinnule fragment(s)
Pteridium aquilinum (L.) Kuhn (bracken)
    pinnule and stalk fragment(s)
Betula sp(p) (birch)
    fruit(s)
cf *Betula* sp(p) (?birch)
    bud(s)/bud-scale(s)
Alnus glutinosa (L.) Gaertner (alder)
    bud(s)/bud-scale(s)
Corylus avellana L. (hazel)
    nut(s)/nutshell fragment(s)
Quercus sp(p) (oak)
    bud(s)/bud-scale(s)
Ficus carica L. (fig)
    seed(s)
Urtica dioica L. (stinging nettle)
    achene(s)
Urtica urens L. (annual nettle)
    achene(s)
Polygonum aviculare agg. (knotgrass)
    fruit(s)
Polygonum hydropiper L. (water-pepper)
    fruit(s)
Polygonum persicaria L. (persicaria/red shank)
    fruit(s)
Polygonum lapathifolium L. (pale persicaria)
    fruit(s)
Bilderdykia convolvulus (L.) Dumort. (black bindweed)
    fruit fragment(s)
Rumex sp(p) (docks)
    fruit(s)
Chenopodium ficifolium Sm. (fig-leaved goosefoot)
    seed(s)
Chenopodium album L. (fat hen)
    seed(s)
Chenopodium sp(p) (goosefoots)
    seed(s)
Atriplex sp(p) (oraches)
    seed(s)
Montia fontana ssp *chondrosperma* (Fenzl) Walters (blinks)
    seed(s)
Stellaria media (L.) Vill. (chickweed)
    seed(s)
Stellaria cf *neglecta* Weihe in Bluff and Fingerh. ?greater chickweed)
    seed(s)
Stellaria graminea L. (lesser stitchwort)
    seed(s)
Sagina sp(p) (pearlworts)   seed(s)
Spergula arvensis L. (corn spurrey)
    seed(s)

Agrostemma githago L. (corncockle)
    seed fragment(s)
Ranunculus Section *Ranunculus*
(meadow/creeping/bulbous buttercup)
    achene(s)
Ranunculus sceleratus L. (celery-leaved
crowfoot)
    achene(s)
Ranunculus flammula L. (lesser spearwort)
    achene(s)
Ranunculus Subgenus *Batrachium* (water
crowfoots)
    achene(s)
Rorippa islandica (Oeder) Borbàs (northern
marsh yellow-cress)
    seed(s)
Brassica rapa L. (turnip)
    seed(s)
Raphanus raphanistrum L. (wild radish)
    pod segments/pod fragment(s)
Rubus idaeus L. (raspberry)
    seed(s)
Rubus fruticosus agg. (blackberry/bramble)
    seed(s)
Rubus/Rosa sp(p) (blackberry, etc/rose)
    prickle(s)
Potentilla anserina L. (silverweed)
    achene(s)
Potentilla cf *erecta* (L.) Räuschel (?tormentil)
    achene(s)
Potentilla cf *reptans* L. (?creeping cinquefoil)
    achene(s)
Aphanes microcarpa (Boiss. and Reuter)
Rothm. (slenderparsley-piert)
    achene(s)
Crataegus sp/*Prunus spinosa* (hawthorn/sloe)
    thorn(s)
Prunus spinosa L. (sloe)
    charred fruitstone(s)
Leguminosae (pea family)
    flower(s)/petal(s)/pod(s)/pod
    fragment(s)
cf *Trifolium pratense* L. (?red clover)
    pod(s) and/pod lid(s)
Linum catharticum L. (purging flax)
    capsule(s)/capsule fragment(s)/
    seed(s)
Ilex aquifolium L. (holly)
    leaf epidermis fragment(s)
Viola sp(p) (violets/pansies, etc)
    seed(s)
Hydrocotyle vulgaris L. (marshpennywort)
    mericarp(s)
Pastinaca sativa L. (wild parsnip)
    mericarp(s)
Ericaceae (heather family)
    leaf/leaves
Calluna vulgaris (L.) Hull (heather, ling)
    flower(s)/seed(s)/shoot
    fragment(s)/twig(s)
cf *Calluna vulgaris* (L.) Hull (?heather, ling)
    root/twig fragment(s)
Vaccinium sp(p) (bilberries)
    seed(s)
Fraxinus excelsior L. (ash)
    wood fragment(s)
Galeopsis Subgenus *Galeopsis* (hemp-nettles)
    nutlet(s)
Prunella vulgaris L. (selfheal)
    nutlet(s)
Lycopus europaeus L. (gipsywort)
    nutlet(s)
Solanum nigrum L. (black nightshade)
    seed(s)
Solanum dulcamara L. (woody nightshade)
    seed(s)
Rhinanthus sp(p) (yellow rattles)
    charred and uncharred seed(s)

Plantago major L. (greater plantain)
    seed(s)
Plantago lanceolata L. (ribwort plantain)
    seed(s)
Sambucus sp(p) (elder, etc)
    seed fragment(s)
Sambucus nigra L. (elder)
    seed(s)
cf *Aster tripolium* L. (?sea aster)
    achene(s)
Achillea millefolium L. (yarrow)
    achene(s)
Carduus/Cirsium sp(p) (thistles)
    achene(s)
Centaurea sp(p) (knapweeds, etc)
    achene fragment(s)
Hypochoeris sp(p) (cat's ears)
    achene(s)
Leontodon sp(p) (hawkbits)
    achene(s)
Sonchus asper (L.) Hill (prickly sow-thistle)
    achene(s)
Taraxacum sp(p) (dandelions)
    achene(s)
cf *Crepis* sp(p) (?hawk's-beards)
    achene(s)
Triglochin maritima L. (sea arrowgrass)
    carpel(s)
Juncus sp(p) (rushes)
    seed(s)
Juncus inflexus/effusus/conglomeratus
(hard/soft/compact rush)
    seed(s)
Juncus squarrosus L. (heath rush)
    seed(s)
Juncus gerardi Loisel. (mud rush)
    seed(s)
Juncus bufonius L. (toad rush)
    seed(s)
Juncus cf *articulatus* L. (?jointed rush)
    seed(s)
Luzula sp(p) (woodrushes)
    seed(s)
cf *Gramineae* (?grasses)
    culm base-rhizome fragment(s)
Gramineae (grasses)
    culm fragment(s)
Gramineae (grasses)
    waterlogged caryopsis/es
Gramineae/Cerealia (grasses/cereals)
    culm node(s)
cf *Triticum* sp(p) (?wheats)
    waterlogged glume-base(s)
Triticum/Secale (wheat/rye)
    waterlogged caryopsis(es)/periderm
    fragments ('bran')
Danthonia decumbens (L.) DC. in Lam. and
DC. (heath grass)
    caryopsis(es),
    spikelets/cleistogenes
cf *Danthonia decumbens* (L.) DC. in Lam. and
DC. (?heath grass)
    cleistogene(s) (basal sterile
    flowers)
Lemna sp(p) (duckweeds) seed(s)
Scirpus lacustris sl (bulrush)
    nutlet(s)
Scirpus setaceus L. (bristle club-rush)
    nutlet(s)
cf *Eriophorum vaginatum* L. (?cotton-grass)
    rhizome and/or stem fragment(s)
Eleocharis palustris sl (common spike-rush)
    nutlet(s)
Carex sp(p) (sedges)
    nutlet(s)

Table 6 Complete list of plant taxa.

101

Taxonomic order and nomenclature for insects follow Kloet and Hincks (1964–77).

Nematoda
Heterodera sp (cyst)
Trichuris sp (egg)

Oligochaeta
Oligochaeta sp (egg capsule)

Arthropoda

Crustacea
Daphnia sp (ephippium)
Cladocera spp (ephippium)
Ostracoda sp

Dermaptera
Dermaptera sp

Hemiptera
Stygnocoris sp oa
Scolopostethus sp oap
Conomelus anceps (Germar) oap
Auchenorhyncha spp oap
Aphidoidea sp
Coccoidea sp
Hemiptera sp (nymph)

Diptera
Bibionidae sp
Syrphidae sp (larva)
Diptera sp (larva)
Diptera spp (pupa)
Diptera spp (puparium)
Diptera spp (adult)

Siphonaptera
Pulex irritans (Linnaeus)

Hymenoptera
Formicidae sp
Proctotrupoidea sp
Hymenoptera Parasitica sp
Hymenoptera sp

Coleoptera
Carabus nemoralis Müller oa
Nebria sp oa
Dyschirius globosus (Herbst) oa
Dyschirius sp indet oa
Trechus obtusus or *quadristriatus* oa
Trechus micros (Herbst) u
Trechus sp indet ob
Asaphidion flavipes (Linnaeus) oa
Bembidion lampros or *properans* oa
Bembidion sp oa
Tachys sp oa
Pterostichus (*Poecilus*) sp oa
Pterostichus sp ob
Calathus sp oa
Agonum sp oa
Amara sp oa
Harpalus rufipes (Degeer) oa
Harpalus sp oa
Acupalpus dubius Schilsky oa
Carabidae spp ob
Haliplidae sp u
Hydroporinae sp oaw
Agabus bipustulatus (Linnaeus) oaw
Colymbetinae sp oaw
Helophorus aquaticus (Linnaeus) oaw

Helophorus tuberculatus Gyllenhal oa
Helophorus spp oaw
Coelostoma orbiculare (Fabricius) oaw
Sphaeridium sp rf
Cercyon analis (Paykull) rt
Cercyon haemorrhoidalis (Fabricius) rf
Cercyon melanocephalus (Linnaeus) rt
Cercyon terminatus (Marsham) rf
Cercyon unipunctatus (Linnaeus) rf
Cercyon sp indet u
Megasternum obscurum (Marsham) rt
Cryptopleurum minutum (Fabricius) rf
?*Anacaena* sp oaw
Laccobius sp oaw
Acritus nigricornis (Hoffmann) rt
Gnathoncus sp rt
Onthophilus striatus (Forster) rt
Histerinae spp u
Ochthebius sp oaw
Ptenidium sp rt
Leiodidae sp u
Micropeplus fulvus Erichson rt
Acidota crenata (Fabricius) oa
Lesteva longoelytrata (Goeze) oad
Phyllodrepa ?*floralis* (Paykull) rt
Omalium ?*rivulare* (Paykull) rt
Omalium sp rt
Omaliinae sp u
Carpelimus ?*bilineatus* Stephens rt
Carpelimus pusillus group u
Carpelimus sp indet u
Platystethus arenarius (Fourcroy) rf
Platystethus cornutus group oad
Platystethus nitens (Sahlberg) oad
Anotylus nitidulus (Gravenhorst) rtd
Anotylus rugosus (Fabricius) rt
Anotylus sculpturatus group rt
Anotylus tetracarinatus (Block) rt
Oxytelus sculptus Gravenhorst rt
Stenus spp u
?*Euaesthetus* sp oa
Lathrobium sp u
Lithocharis ochracea (Gravenhorst) rt
Rugilus orbiculatus (Paykull) rt
Paederinae sp u
Othius myrmecophilus Kiesenwetter rt
Othius sp rt
Leptacinus sp rt
Gyrohypnus angustatus Stephens rt
Gyrohypnus fracticornis (Müller) rt
Xantholinus glabratus (Gravenhorst) rt
Xantholinus linearis (Olivier) rt
Xantholinus longiventris Heer rt
Xantholinus linearis or *longiventris* rt
Neobisnius sp u
Erichsonius sp u
Philonthus spp u
Gabrius sp rt
Quedius boops group u
Quedius sp u
Staphylininae spp indet u
Tachyporus spp u
Tachinus ?*signatus* Gravenhorst u
Tachinus sp u
Cordalia obscura (Gravenhorst) rt
Falagria caesa or *sulcatula* rt
Falagria or *Cordalia* sp rt
?*Aleochara* sp u
Aleocharinae spp u
Lucanus cervus (Linnaeus) l
Geotrupes sp oarf
Aphodius ?*ater* (Degeer) oarf
Aphodius granarius (Linnaeus) obrf
Aphodius prodromus (Brahm) obrf
Aphodius spp obrf
Onthophagus sp oarf
Hoplia philanthus Illiger oa
Phyllopertha horticola (Linnaeus) oap

Melolonthinae/Rutelinae/Cetoninae sp indet oap
Cyphon sp oad
Byrrhidae sp oap
Dryops sp oad
Ctenicera cuprea (Fabricius) oap
Agriotes sp oap
Elateridae sp (larva)
Elateridae sp ob
Cantharidae sp ob
Anobium punctatum (Degeer) l
Kateretes sp oapd
Brachypterus sp oap
Meligethes sp oap
Omosita colon (Linnaeus) rt
Omosita colon or *discoidea* rt
Rhizophagus sp u
Monotoma picipes Herbst rt
Monotoma sp indet rt
Cryptolestes ferrugineus (Stephens) g
Oryzaephilus surinamensis (Linnaeus) g
Cryptophagus spp rd
Atomaria sp rd
Ephistemus globulus (Paykull) rd
Phalacridae sp oap
Cerylon sp l
Orthoperus sp rt
Stephostethus lardarius (Degeer) rt
Lathridius minutus group rd
Enicmus sp rt
Corticaria sp rt
Corticarina or *Cortinicara* sp rt
Typhaea stercorea (Linnaeus) rd
Aglenus brunneus (Gyllenhal) rt
Palorus ?ratzeburgi (Wissman) g
Tenebrio obscurus Fabricius rt
Anthicus floralis or *formicarius* rt
Bruchinae sp u
Gastrophysa viridula (Degeer) oap
Hydrothassa sp oadp
Chrysomelinae sp oap
Longitarsus sp oap
Altica sp oap
Chaetocnema arida group oap
Chaetocnema concinna (Marsham) oap
Chaetocnema sp indet oap
Cassida ?flaveola Thunberg oap
Apion sp oap
Otiorhynchus sp oap
Sitona sp oap
Alophus triguttatus (Fabricius) oap
Sitophilus granarius (Linnaeus) g
Limnobaris ?pilistriata (Stephens) oapd
Curculionidae sp oa
Scolytidae sp l
Coleoptera sp (larva)
Coleoptera sp u

Arachnida
Acarina sp
Aranae sp

Table 7 Complete list of invertebrate taxa.

Context	Sample	Action	Tub num' sampled	Notes	Parasite squash
79	1004	1kg w/o	1		
88	1016	1kg w/o	1 of 2	voucher tub 1, NFA on tub 2	
148	1040	1kg flot	1 of 3	NFA other 2 tubs, voucher tub 1	x
160	1021	BS all	1		
174	1100	1kg flot	1 of 2	tub 1 NFA, tub 2 voucher	
216	110201	1kg flot	1 of 2	different from tub 2, voucher tub 1	x
216	110202	1 kg flot	2 of 2	different from tub 1, voucher tub 2	x
216	110202	Wood	2 of 2	included in sample	
216	131611	1kg flot	1 of 3	organic component of sample, tubs 2 and 3 NFA	x
216	131612	1kg flot	1 of 3	clay component of sample, voucher tub 1	x
222	111001	1kg flot	1 of 3	tub 3 NFA, voucher tub 1	x
222	111002	none yet	2 of 3	different from other tubs but NFA	
227	1111	1kg flot	1 of 2		
237	1109	1kg flot	3 of 3	check numbers of tubs 1 and 2, voucher tub 3	
279	1103	1kg flot and BS of excess	1		
330	124903	1kg flot	3 of 4	tubs 1 and 4 NFA; tub 2 NFA, voucher tub 3	
330	124904	1kg flot	4 of 4	done by mistake as an extra, voucher tub 4	
338	124701	none	1 of 5	tubs 2, 4, and 5 same but NFA	
338	124702	none	2 of 5	same as 1,4, and 5	
338	124703	1kg flot	3 of 5	different from 1, 2, 4, and 5, voucher tub 3	x
339	1248	none	2 of 3	NFA on all	
362	1317	1kg flot	1 of 2	tub 2 NFA, voucher tub 1	x
409	1250	1kg w/o	1 of 1	voucher	
425	1251	1kg flot	1 of 1	voucher	x
430	1252	none	1 of 1	NFA	
431	1253(T1)	1kg flot	1		
431	1253(T2)	4.85kg w/o			
443	1254	8kg BS	1 of 1		x
448	1255	1kg w/o	1 of 1	voucher	
450	1256	1kg flot	1 of 2	voucher tub 1, tub 2 NFA	x
462	1315	none	1 of 1	on hold	

Table 8 Biological samples from Dowbridge Close, Kirkham: action taken. NFA: no further action

Phase	Context	Object No.	Species	Element	Comments
1:1	17	1023	Indet	Fragments	Three tiny burnt fragments
1:2	229	1176	Sheep/Goat	Tibia	Distal end, burnt, ep fused
			Indet	Fragments	10 small burnt fragments
1:3	230	1181	Cattle	Tooth	Fragments
1:4	11	1048	Indet	Fragment	Burnt
1:4	70	1077	Indet	Fragment	Burnt
1:4	79	1083	Indet	Fragments	Four small burnt fragments
1:4	88	1090	Cattle	Tooth	Fragments enamel
1:4	160	1153	Indet	Fragment	Probably tiny fragment of cattle tooth enamel
1:4	437	1331	Cattle	Femur	Proximal shaft, canid gnawing
2:2	370	1289	Indet	Fragment	Burnt
3:3	355	1321	Indet	Fragments	Wet decayed, large animal
3:3	371	1298	Cattle	Tooth	Fragments enamel
			Cattle	Phalanx	Burnt fragment distal end
			Indet	Fragments	Almost completely decayed
3:3	371	1297	Dog	Ulna	Shaft, curious notch distal end
3:3	371	1381	Dog	Skeleton	Skull Jaw L + R Scap R DF Hum L + R PFDF Rad L + R PFDF Uln L + R PFDF Vt x 4 CFAF Vl x 5 CFAF Rib x 16 PF
2 or 3	139	1150	Indet	Fragments	Two tiny burnt fragments
Modern	3	1009	Indet	Fragment	Burnt
Modern	127	1134	Cattle	Patella	Poor condition
Modern	224	1188	Indet	Fragment	Burnt fragments
Modern	287	1216	Indet	Fragment	Burnt
Modern	321	1231	Cattle	Tooth	Fragments enamel

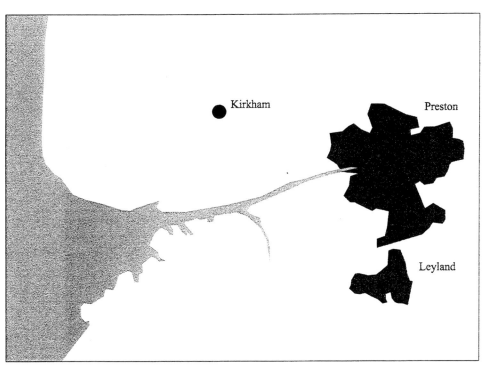
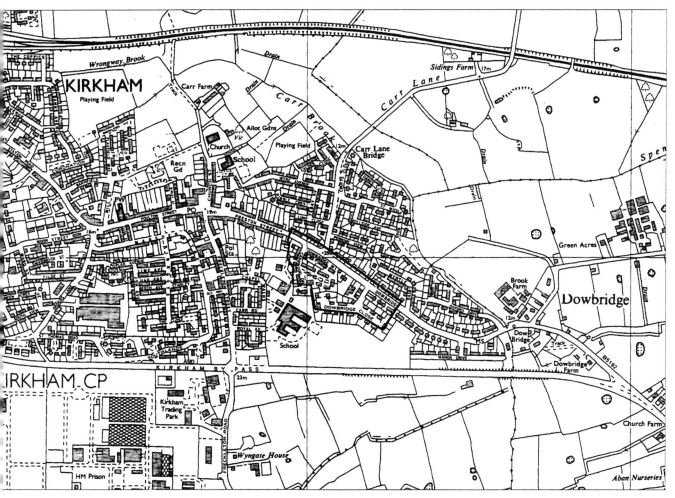

Figure 1 : Site Location

Fig 2 : Trench Location Plan

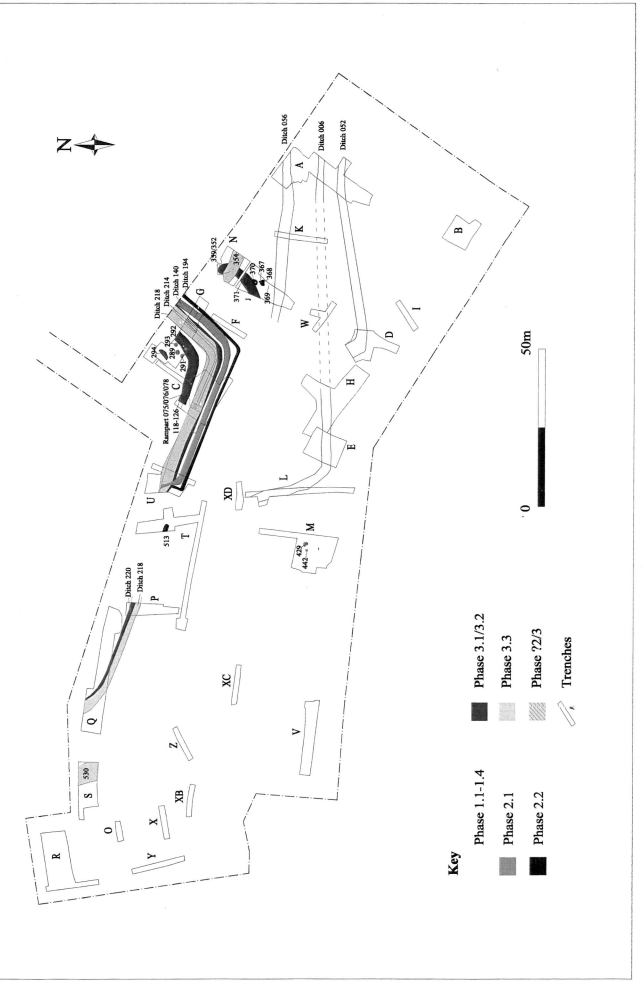

Figure 3 : All Phases of Site

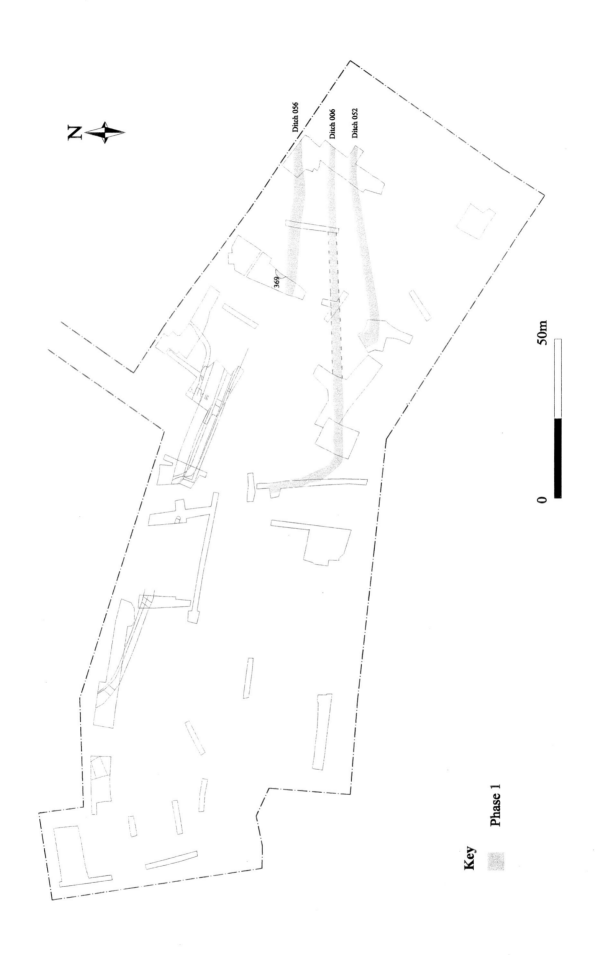

N

Ditch 056
Ditch 006
Ditch 052

369

Key

Phase 1

0   50m

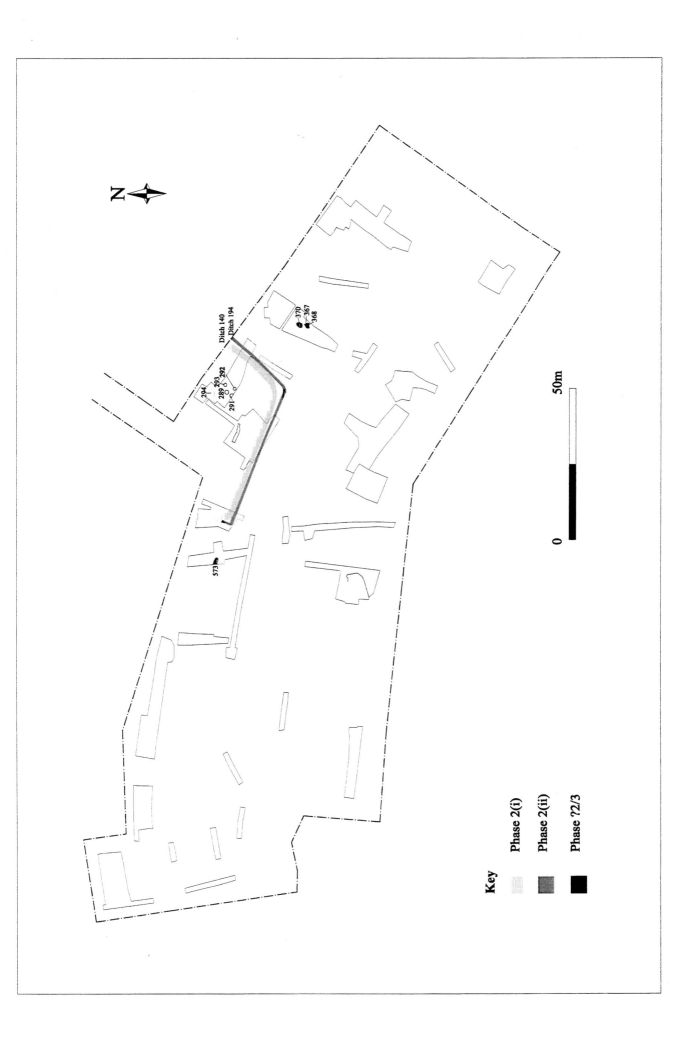

Figure 5 : Phase 2 Activity

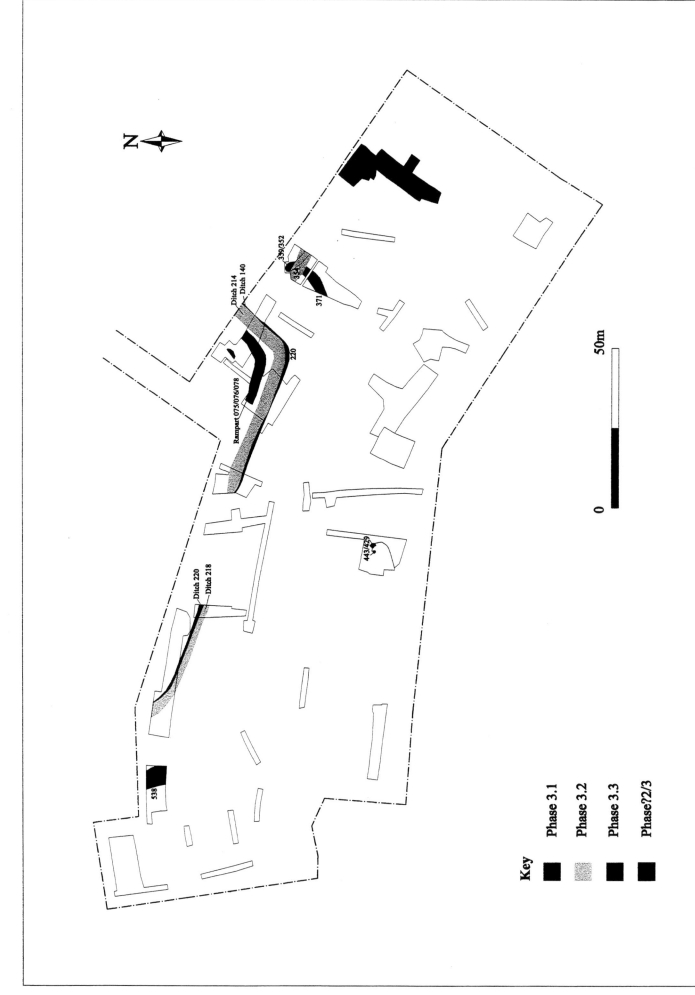

Fig 6 : Phase 3 and 2/3 Activity

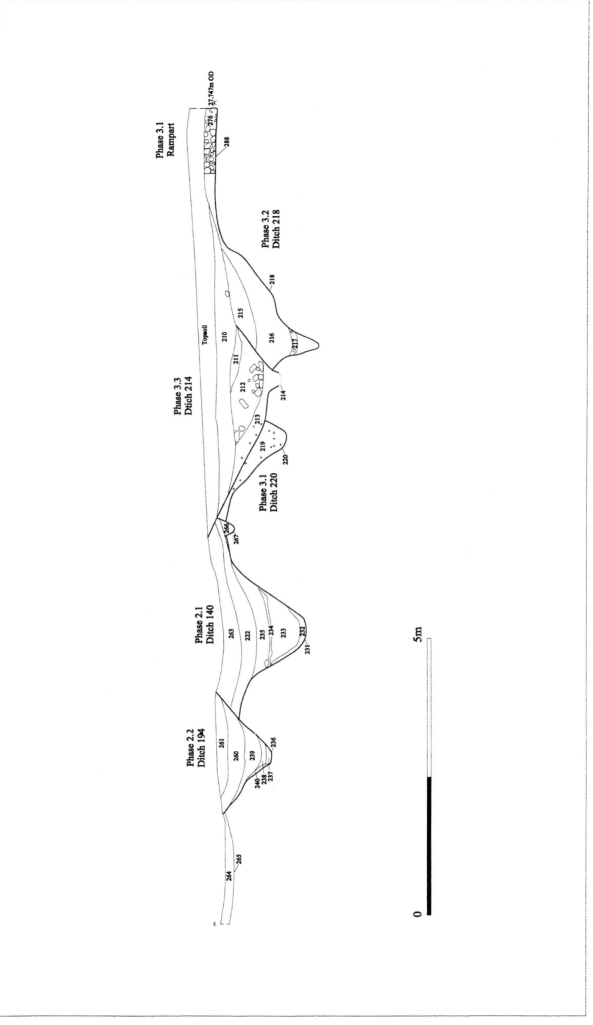

Fig 7 : Section through Ditches

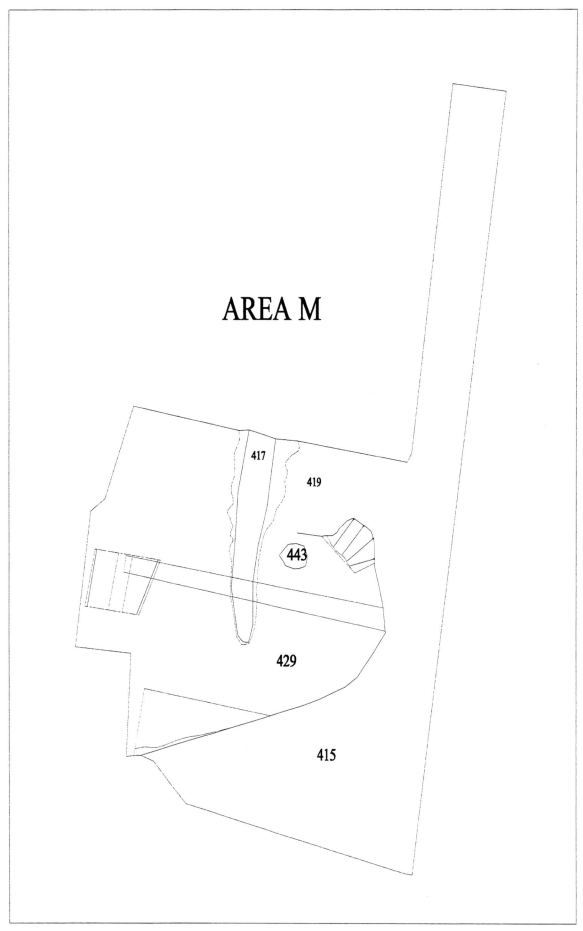

AREA M

417

419

443

429

415

Fig 8 : Detail of Industrial Activity : Phase 2/3

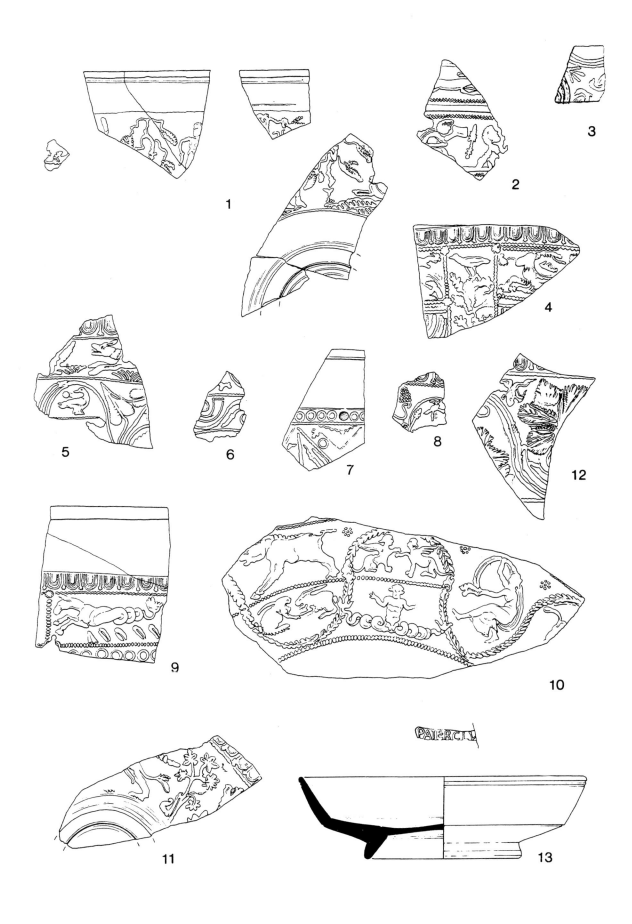

Figure 9: Samian vessels

Scale 1:1

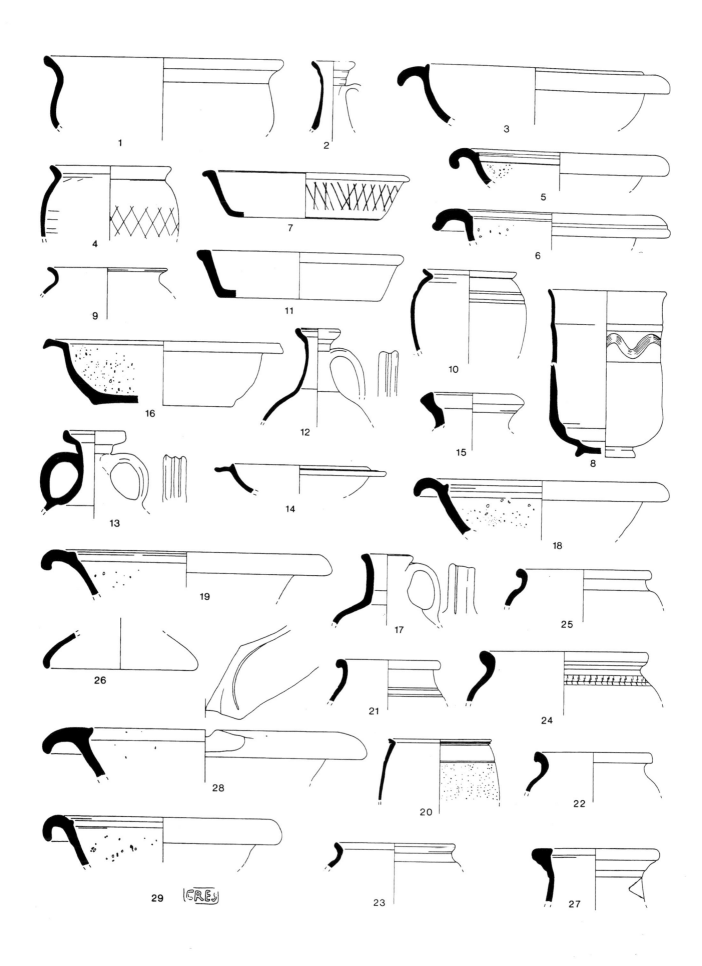

Figure 10: Roman coarse pottery
Scale 1:4

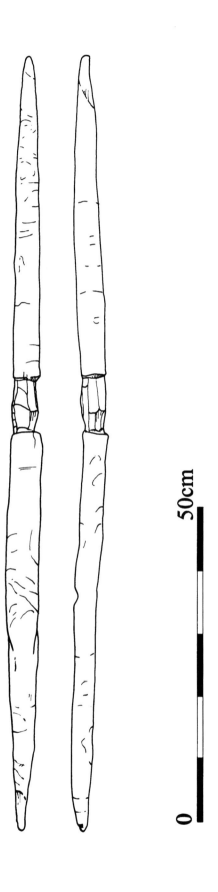

Figure 11: *The Pilum Muralis*

Plate 1: Altar depiciting three mother goddesses, now forming the font at St John's Church, Lund, believed to be found under the line of the Roman road from Ribchester to Kirkham (DCA Shotter)

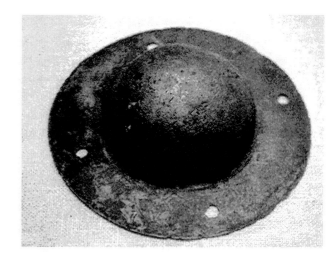

Plate 2: Shield boss found in a small stream adjoining New England Spring in 1800. The original is in the British Museum (DCA Shotter)

Plate 3: Excavations begin at Dowbridge: Trench A

Plate 4: Ditches of temporary camps cutting the natural subsoil

Plate 5: Phase 1.4: Ditch 056

Plate 6: Phase 1.4: Ditch 056, showing a change in the shape of its profile

Plate 7: Phase 2.1: Ditch 140, southern return of circuit about the fortlet

Plate 8: Phase 2.2: Ditch 513, the possible *titulus*

Plate 9: The remains of the stone wall fort, showing the proximity of the stones to the present day ground surface

Plate 10: Phase 3.1: Wall 075, the rampart revetment

Plate 11: Phase 3.1: Wall 294, the inner rampart revetment

Plate 12: Phase 3.1: Wall 277, the inner rampart revetment

Plate 13: Phase 3.1: Close up of Wall 075, tumble from the rampart revetment

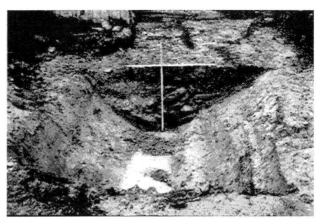

Plate 14: Phase 3.3: Ditch 421, the last re-cut of the stone fort ditch

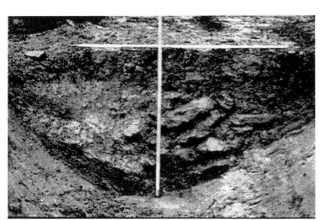

Plate 15: Phase 3.3: Ditch 421, detail of tumble from the stone wall fort

Plate 16: The *Pilum Muralis in situ*